SEXUAL DEVELOPMENT

OF

YOUNG CHILDREN

Virginia Lively, M.S.
Kindergarten Teacher
&
Edwin Lively, Ph.D.
Sociologist

 Delmar Publishers Inc. ®

NOTICE TO THE READER

Cover design by Nancy Gworek
Cover art by Ron Young

Delmar Staff

Administrative Editor: Jay Whitney
Project Editor: Carol Micheli
Production Supervisor: Larry Main
Art Supervisor: John Lent
Design Supervisor: Susan C. Mathews

For information, address Delmar Publishers Inc.
2 Computer Drive West, Box 15-015
Albany, New York 12212

Printed in the United States of America
Published simultaneously in Canada
by Nelson Canada,
a division of The Thomson Corporation

10 9 8 7 6 5 4 3 2 1

Library of Congress Cataloging-in-Publication Data

Lively, Virginia.
    Sexual development of young children/Virginia Lively & Edwin Lively.
        p. cm.
    Includes bibliographical references.
    ISBN 0-8273-4198-9
        1. Sex instruction -- United States. 2. Children -- United States --
Sexual behavior. I. Lively, Edwin. II. Title.
HQ57.5.A3L58 1991
306.7'083 -- dc20

TABLE OF CONTENTS

VIII. APPENDICES

FOREWORD

I have always hoped that teachers would do more writing, sharing their insight into children and families, their wisdom needed to bring about improvement in the future. I know from the many workshops that I conduct with teachers around the country that there is a deep reservoir of knowledge that lies, largely untapped, in our teaching profession. So often, in workshops, I have urged teachers to write articles, write books.

<u>Sexual Development of Young Children</u> is just the kind of book that I have been hoping for. Virginia Lively is a kindergarten teacher; her husband, Edwin Lively, a sociologist. Together, they make quite a team.

One of the most wonderful aspects of this book is that it is rooted in an everyday knowledge of young children and how they develop and their overall, as well as their sexual development. Rich case studies of children, sometimes including children's drawings, abound, bringing the more theoretical points home with an often unforgettable poignancy. Always, the authors convey a profound respect for all concerned-children, parents, and teachers. Unfortunately, that respect is unusual - those who advocate for children or teachers sometimes blame parents, but such is thankfully not the case here.

<u>Sexual Development of Young Children</u> offers practical suggestions on topics as diverse as helping the child have a positive image as a male or female to more controversial issues that range from addressing questions of how babies are conceived and born to sexual abuse and AIDS.

This book will help parents and teachers understand many of the "whys" of sexuality (why children have the misunderstandings they do, for example) and learn how to build a strong and open communication between adults and children. The Livelys have said it best in their conclusion: "Be ever aware that you cannot avoid communicating to the young child. You communicate by speaking and also by not speaking; by what you say and what you don't say."

This book will help adults learn and grow. For "In the final sense, helping young children build a strong sexuality means helping them enjoy being children who are also willing to grow up."

Ellen Galinsky
Co-President, The Families and Work Institute
Co-Author, <u>The Preschool Year</u>
January 11, 1990

AUTHOR'S PREFACE

Sexual Development of Young Children had its origin when the senior author chose to write a paper on young children while enrolled in a graduate seminar on Sexuality. Such a paper proved to be impractical because of the paucity of material on the topic. The information available in textbooks, professional journals, and research monographs was devoted primarily to the sexuality of teenagers and young adults and to patterns of deviancy in the area. Subsequently, the authors set out to write a paper on the sexuality of young children, which grew into a monograph, and ultimately, this book. In addition to the difficulties in researching the subject and extrapolating a great deal of the information available in a variety of disciplines, there was also the task of reconciling the practical and personalized approach of a kindergarten teacher with the more theoretical and statistical interests of a sociologist. The results as they appear in this book are satisfying, but they were not achieved without effort.

The book is designed for use as a textbook or resource book in either lower or upper level college courses in human development, child development, early childhood education, socialization, and family development. It is also appropriate for use by anyone who plans to or is working with young children such as the staff members of public and private kindergartens and the lower elementary grades, plus those persons involved in Day Care Centers, Headstart Programs, Nursery Schools, and After-School Care Programs. Others who may find the book informative and worthwhile are Social Workers, the personnel in Juvenile Delinquency Centers, and Pediatric Nurses. Furthermore, the academic aspects such as citing references and briefly presenting some theoretical approaches should not prevent parents and parents-to-be from attaining insights and recommendations as they seek to understand their offspring and pursue the multi-faceted task of preparing them for adolescence and adulthood. The Resource section in the Appendix containing a list of Hot Lines and suggested readings for specific purposes should prove useful for a variety of needs. In fact, the authors frequently utilized several of the Hot Lines to obtain current publications and up-to-date statistics.

The wide variety of material presented, in part through the use of children's vignettes, is designed to illustrate the reactions and thought processes of young children. Their small stature forces them to view the world by looking at knees, belts, and window sills; they see things from a different perspective than adults. Limitations on experience cause them to define things differently than grownups. For similar reasons, they express themselves verbally and behaviorally in non-adult ways. The most effective relationships with young children require an appreciation of these differences and an ability to recognize and work with them. The vignettes are valuable for giving the child a voice in what they see and feel as their sexuality develops. This is also true of the children's drawings which are presented in the book. More than anything else, the vignettes and drawings reveal the awareness of young children about males and females, about young people and adults, and especially about growing up.

The authors wish to express their sincere appreciation for the support of family, friends, and colleagues throughout the preparation of the book. Specifically, we want to mention Jacob Schapiro, Ph.D, of SCORE, for his wise counsel and professional expertise; Barbara Somerville, of the West Palm Beach Post, for her encouragement; Ellen Galinsky, for agreeing to write a Forward in the midst of a busy schedule, and the Book Reviewers for their many positive comments and helpful suggestions. Finally we have had the assistance of Jay Whitney, ECE Editor for Delmar Publishers, who was always supportive, and of Richard Murdoch and Tricia Martin, who helped prepare the manuscript and put it in final form. Finally, if this book is as helpful as we intend it to be, some young children will be better off than they would without it.

DEDICATION

With grateful appreciation for all
we have learned from them, we dedicate this book
to our children,
Lynn, Geri, and Eddie;
and to our grandchildren;
Dan, Bethany, Brooke, and Britney;
and to all young children throughout the world
with the hope that the world will become a
healthier and happier place in which to grow up.

Virginia and Edwin Lively

CHAPTER 1

INTRODUCTION TO THE SEXUALITY OF YOUNG CHILDREN

Vern and Amy

After a Christmas Vacation in Florida, Mrs. Elkin initiated a new unit on sea animals in her kindergarten class. The children's fascination with her account of seeing a whale swimming in the ocean encouraged her to read them a story about whales. The characteristics of whales as presented in the book included the fact that they are mammals, with one of the illustrations showing a baby whale nursing from its mother's breast. After seeing the picture, Vern, a very intelligent and verbal child, stated that he knew that whales were mammals. He said he knew because he had grown inside his mother's body and gotten milk from his mother's breast just like the baby whale.

Amy listened intently to the discussion with Vern and later began to look at the book on whales. Finally she brought it to Mrs. Elkin to ask if Vern was right that babies really grow inside their mother's bodies. When Mrs. Elkin answered yes, the little girl replied that that was bad. The teacher had been alerted to the possibility that Amy might encounter problems during the year by Amy's mother. She emphasized that she believed children should be taught modesty, and she did not want any situations to occur in which Amy's underclothing might be exposed. Amy must not sit on the floor and must always wear slacks when she went to the playground.

Mrs. Elkin was already aware that Amy avoided any play situation in which she might show her underwear. One day she became hysterical in the classroom when she tripped and went sprawling on the floor. Sobbing, she told the teacher that she was bad because some of the children had seen her underclothes. She said her mother had told her many times that under her panties was a bad part of her body, a place where bad things happen and people do bad things to each other. She added that she never touched herself on the bad part because her mother had told her not to do so. The teacher arranged a conference with the mother and explained in detail what had happened when Amy fell and how upset the little girl had become because she believed her panties had been exposed to the other children.

After some discussion, the mother revealed, hesitantly, that she had been raped by a neighbor when she was eight years of age and that she had some very strong feelings in the area of sex. At the same time, she said she did not want her child to be unhappy and asked Mrs. Elkin to arrange for some help, saying, "I believe I need some guidance, because I am creating problems for Amy." The mother agreed to confer with the school psychologist and such a meeting was arranged. After several conferences, the mother agreed that Amy should be released from the restrictions on clothing and that certain types of behavior could be modified.

In this actual incident, Vern and Amy and all the other children in the class experienced another piece in the development of their sexuality. Vern and Amy did not enter the discussion of whales and other mammals with the same background. The teacher's presentation and the pictures did not mean the same thing to Amy that they did to Vern. How it will affect their attitudes and behaviors in the future is unknown but it will have an effect. This is the nature of growth and development of sexuality. It begins at birth and continues through life, and every incident has the possibility of being significant for the future.

YOUNG CHILDREN GROWING UP

Persons who guide and work with young children need accurate and up-to-date information about sexuality in general, how it develops, and especially its applicability to infants and young children. This is necessary in order to be constructive and to give proper and useful assistance. It is quite disruptive and may be detrimental at times when approaches to human sexuality are developed under such labels as "sex education" or "sex instruction" but then distorted by emotional and/or moralistic influences. In such cases, if what is presented is inaccurate, incomplete, or inadequately presented because of a bias or lack of information, the most useful effects are negated. This is true whether information comes from a parent, teacher, or other well-meaning person.

The young child today is living in a society in which sex and sexuality are emphasized in a variety of ways and to a greater degree than ever before. When you examine any non-fiction best seller list, a large number of the leading books will be related, directly or indirectly, to sex and sexual behavior. This is even more true of the best sellers on the fiction list, the most popular TV programs and movies, and many magazines on the news stands. If this popularity is an indicator of people's interests, then adolescents, adults, and many seniors are not only concerned with the sexuality of others, but equally of themselves. Unfortunately, interest and concern do not necessarily coincide with knowledge and understanding; this is one of the major purposes of this book - to reduce the distance between them.

A young child's sexuality continuously develops in, around, and beyond the home and the classroom. Therefore teachers, as well as parents, are giving guidance to the children around them whether they do it consciously or not. On the other hand, a review of the literature suggests that little attention has been given to the development of the sexuality of the young child. Although there is a substantial amount of literature on sexuality in general, including research reports and controlled studies, very little can be found that is devoted to the infant and young child. Numerous discussions with both the parents of young children and their teachers reveals that neither group is well-informed on the subject and most will, off the record, admit to a real sense of inadequacy in guiding the young people with whom they are associated.

Inasmuch as parents and teachers are so intimately involved in the continuous development of young children's sexuality, it is not a topic they can avoid and they should not attempt to do so. Questions will be asked; situations will arise; and most importantly of all, the child will continue to mature: mentally, physically, and sexually. All those who work with the child will find it necessary to react to the fact of being and doing plus continuing growth over time, and the most helpful approach will be the one that is honest, accurate, and applicable to the current situation.

Cassandra

During kindergarten playtime, Cassandra confided to the teacher that her mother had "missed" getting a new baby at the hospital the day before.

"My mommy never said she was going to the hospital to get a baby but that is where Grandma said she was going." Cassandra hesitated, then asked, "Miss Fritsch, how do you miss a baby in the hospital?"

Miss Fritsch, her discomfort quite apparent, told Cassandra, "I'm too busy to talk right now."

A child who overheard the conversation said, "The baby was in your mother's stomach. Don't you even know that?"

Deciding that something was mysterious and complicated about how babies are born, Cassandra gave up trying to find out, but she continued to think about her mother and the "missed" baby.

The teacher missed an opportunity to ease the child's mind about life, babies, and the fact that nature is not always perfect. Cassandra was ready for an introduction to the reproductive process, not in detail, but a few honest statements about mothers and babies. The next vignette introduces still a different situation involving a young child and sexual health.

Ara

As Mrs. Allen passed by her five year old daughter's open bedroom door, she noticed her child, Ara, fondling her genitals. When she entered the bedroom, feeling quite uncomfortable, the mother attempted to deal with the situation by asking, "Why are you doing that Ara? Are you sore or are your pants too tight?" The child replied very simply, "No, I'm just rubbing myself." Mrs. Allen's response was to advise her daughter in a matter-of-fact way that such behavior was considered by people to be a private matter and was not approved by other people.

Feeling quite inadequate, she patted the youngster and left the room.

Cassandra's teacher did not attempt to cope with the situation while Ara's mother did. In both cases there was an opportunity to educate the child about a part of the developing human sexuality. It is not easy to explain miscarriage or a sensual feeling in the genitals, but they are real. Miss Fritsch would have been quite in order to comment briefly on birth and occasional accidents and then refer the matter to the parents for a fuller explanation. Mrs. Allen could have gone on to explain personal as well as private behavior and the importance of protecting one's body from others. In these kinds of incidents, it is important to avoid creating any type of guilt feelings about behavior or embarrassment with regard to situations, and still provide some guidance.

Teddy

Late in September, the pupils in a kindergarten class were asked to draw a picture of a person. This is a technique used to determine the perceptiveness of a child to the environment; in this case, the awareness of people and their characteristics. The children were told that their pictures would be put on the bulletin board after each child had talked about his picture and they would be left there for parent's night.

Teddy drew a rather detailed picture of a man which included a large penis and a mass of pubic hair. (See Figure 1-1) The reactions of three teachers is described below; one of which is the one that did occur and the other two are hypothetical.

TEACHER A

She saw the drawing before it was shown to the class. She told Teddy it was not a nice drawing, tore it up, and gave him a piece of paper on which to make another one. The little boy was also instructed to cover the person with clothes where he should be covered. Later, when asked to comment on his new drawing, Teddy reluctantly said that it was his Daddy and made no further remarks.

TEACHER B

She collected all the pictures after each child had discussed his own drawing. When one child asked Teddy why he had put a "pee-wee" on his picture, the teacher turned to talk to another child before the boy could

Figure 1-1 My daddy by Teddy, age five

answer. The next day all the pictures were on the bulletin board except Teddy's. When asked about it, the teacher appeared quite surprised and then apologized to Teddy for having lost his drawing.

TEACHER C

She also collected the drawings after each child had an opportunity to tell about his own effort. However when Teddy was questioned about the inclusion of a penis, she waited for his answer. He explained that all boys have penises so he put one on his person. All the pictures were then placed on the bulletin board where they remained until after parent's night. Although there were no names on the drawings, Teddy proudly pointed his out to his mother and father who proceeded to praise him for his excellent picture.

Certainly Teddy and all the other children would be affected differently by the reaction of the teacher. Teacher A showed emotion and embarrassment, scolded the child, and destroyed his picture, all of which would affect the child's social development in the area of sexuality by establishing a negative interpretation. Teacher B remained calm but attempted to minimize the situation and then surreptitiously and dishonestly omitted the picture from the display. Perhaps the major failure in this case was the unwillingness or inability to seize the opportunity to guide the child toward a better understanding of what was done and what it meant to people. Teacher C made the most of the incident by accepting the child's effort at self-expression and ego development without creating undue emphasis on Teddy's approach. The differing treatment by the three teachers illustrates how the socialization of teachers has continuing impact in the classroom. Those teachers whose preparation for awareness of the developing sexuality of young children is inadequate or incomplete will sometimes fail to seize opportunities to help the children at the appropriate time.

Julie

In a similar situation, Julie's picture was displayed on a bulletin board along with those of other children. (See Figure 1-2) As can be noted in the accompanying reproduction, her drawing illustrates the little girl's interpretation of her mother before she had her baby. When Julie commented on her picture, she explained that her sister was now two weeks old but before she was born, she was in her mother's stomach. Another child in the class argued with Julie, claiming that the picture showed the mother holding the baby in her arms. Julie insisted the baby was inside her mother and then asked the teacher

Julie was a child who lead many informal discussions and contributed information to the children in her group. The next day after the discussion of her drawing, she brought a picture of her baby sister's sonogram to school. She asked the teacher if she could show and explain the picture to the children. She explained that this was a picture which was taken while her sister was still inside her mother. The children showed varying degrees of interest. One child asked why the picture was taken and how it was made, but her mother went to the hospital to get it. She also explained her mother told her it was to find out if the baby's head was down the way it should be to be born.

Figure 1-2   Mother with unborn child by Julie, age five

to explain how the baby came out. The children all waited for the teacher to answer.

Here again, we have a situation in which different children have different degrees of understanding about one aspect of sexuality, namely, childbearing. How should the teacher utilize this opportunity to expand these young children's awareness of the processes of life? Should the explanation be factual and detailed, with the appropriate modification to the children's level? How should the concept of the uterus be introduced? Is it appropriate for the teacher to refer the matter to the parents for clarification? There are no simple answers to these questions and many others that could be raised because both teachers and parents differ in their ability and willingness to discuss the issues involved. Some would do an excellent job of following up on the matter, some would ignore or distort the questions and thus provide no help to the child, while some would be angry or annoyed that such a situation arose even in the kindergarten. It is also a fact that in some school systems, teachers are forbidden to get into matters of sex education unless it is specifically provided for in the curriculum. Certainly children six years of age and under vary considerably in interest, knowledge, and ability to grasp the nature and importance of the reproduction process. The primary consideration, however, is the utilization of spontaneous situations to clarify something for these youngsters. Occurrences similar to the ones presented here do arise and curiosity will exist; it seems like the proper moment to provide some answers. The nature of the answers depends on the nature of the situation and the capabilities of the teacher.

In the following vignette, the teacher displayed an awareness of her childrens' location, and an ability to size up a difficult situation promptly. She communicated with the concerned persons and also sought to protect the child.

Betsy

Several times during the school year, the kindergarten teacher sent six-year old Betsy to the furnace room to get the custodian to come and correct a situation that he could best handle. One day the teacher missed the little girl and began to search for her. After a while she saw Betsy come out of the furnace room and run to join the other children on the playground.

When the teacher asked where she had been, Betsy said she had gone to the furnace room to see her friend, the custodian. She then said that the regular custodian was sick and was not in the furnace room but a nice friend of his was there doing the work. Betsy added, "I got to sit on his lap and he hugged and kissed me because I was so pretty. He asked me to come back so he could kiss me again on my pretty lips." The teacher knew that Betsy often indulged in fantasy but she also knew that there was a substitute custodian. She was also concerned because the child was in the furnace room for such a long time, and further, that Betsy's story was more hesitant than it would have been if she had been bragging. If the incident had occurred as described it called for prompt action to protect the child, but if it was not true, the substitute's reputation could be seriously damaged.

Inasmuch as the teacher was the first person to become aware of a potentially serious problem, her handling of it was extremely critical for all concerned. In this case, the principal was informed of the incident and decided to remove the substitute custodian's name from the list of those approved for future employment. The parents were informed of the event and told that the adult involved would no longer be present at the school. It was agreed by all that no further action was called for as the child was not harmed and was unaware of the implications for the future. However, it can be asked whether the potential danger may have been transferred to some other school and its pupils at some time in the future. At the present time, most states require that such incidents be reported to the proper authorities.

The stories and anecdotes used in this and the other chapters are derived from actual incidents but have been modified to protect the persons involved. They have been compiled from the files of the authors and other teachers, from parents, from various professionals who work with young children in playground situations, day care centers and nurseries. Parents have been an especially valuable source because of their interest and concern with the development of their children's sexuality, although they were often unfamiliar of that term and its meaning. The cases that have been chosen for inclusion in this book are those that represent everyday situations that happen to children and teachers and parents, regardless of social or economic status or location in a city or state. Some call for action to prevent more serious consequences. All point to the need for communication among all those persons who have a stake in the well-being of the young child.

MALE AND FEMALE

Perhaps the initial concern of new parents is "Is it a girl or a boy?"

Then come the concerns as to the well-being of mother and child. Ultimately questions as to weight, coloring, resemblance to others, and various problems associated with the delivery will be asked. There are no right or wrong answers to such questions but there are definitely preferred answers on the part of many people. The father may want a son, the grandparents want a daughter, some would like the child to look like one side of the family or the other. Sometimes such preferences can be inferred from the name given the child, as when a boy's name is given to a girl, or perhaps a modification of a boy's name. Such preferences can be identified by the way the child is dressed, by the toys given to him or her, or by the kinds of activities that are approved or disapproved. Today the sex of the child can often be determined before delivery but the interest and concern and definite preferences are still present. It is also possible to influence the sex of the child at the time of conception but this is not a common practice at the present time.

At birth, every human child, with few exceptions, can be identified as male or female. The determination of the sex occurs at conception when an X-Y combination of chromosomes results in a male child, and an X-X combination produces a female. The combination that occurs is strictly by chance unless steps are taken to control it, but there are some exceptions or aberrations in the physical characteristics and in the resulting behaviors. At the time of birth, the male is determined visually as having a penis and scrotum and the female as having a vulva. Ultimately the male will develop a beard, some body hair, and a lowering of his voice, while the female will develop functional breasts, broader hips, and the capability of being fertilized by the male's sperm, and carrying and delivering a baby. This female capability becomes real when the menstrual cycle begins, usually in the first years of the teens. At approximately the same age, the male acquires the capability of impregnating the female so she can become a mother. The nature of human beings therefore requires both males and females in order to reproduce and continue the human race from generation to generation. One important focal point in this book is the exploration of the sexual variations among males and females and the impact on the sexual health and development of young children. The dependence on males and females for survival has not prevented conflict, jealousy, and arguments about the relative importance of each sex. There has been research by scholars into questions of significant differences and similarities among males and females in emotional, psychological, neurological, physiological, and intellectual traits or qualities but substantive evidence and general acceptance of specific comparisons is still lacking.

INFANCY AND THE BEGINNING OF SEXUALITY

The first impact on the sexuality of the newborn child is the kind of care received from those who provide for various needs during infancy. As the baby is fed, bathed, clothed, and toilet trained it will learn respect for the body, that bodily sensations are pleasant, and that bodily functions are natural and necessary. This is imparted by the caretaker's attitudes and actions while taking care of the infant. If the nurturing people are supportive and loving, the child begins positive socialization as the emotional and physical needs are met.

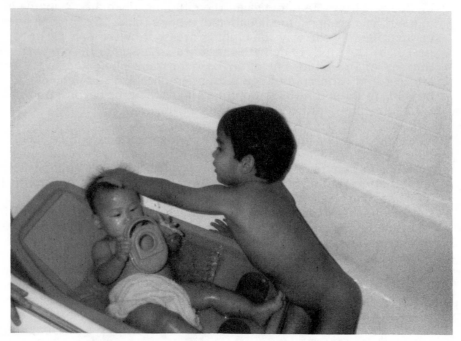

Figure 1-3 *(Photo courtesy of Virginia Lively)*

For the first two years of a child's life, there are three attainments that are necessary for the most effective intellectual, social, and emotional development: to construct a world of permanent objects, to establish a sense of trust, and to attach themselves to the "significant others." It is during this period that the child begins to identify with the caretakers and to learn to establish a relationship which is a vital and necessary component of a healthy sexuality. Whittlestone (1980) says the developmental processes involved in growth and maturation are sensitive to somato-sensory stimulation from the first hours and days of a newborn child.

Out of necessity, the newborn child is so very demanding that parenthood creates a partnership between parent and child. Normally, babies form deep emotional attachments to those who fulfill the daily needs, usually the mother and father and older siblings, and in some cases a "baby-sitter" or equivalent. Infants and young children turn to such a person or persons when they are hungry, disturbed, or playful. Even children who are neglected, abused, and starved tend to remain loyal and trusting of these people and support them with love and attention.

The theory of bonding asserts an attachment between parent and child that begins at birth and develops during the first eighteen months of a child's life. Proponents believe that the child who does not build an attachment, i.e., bond, has a high probability of not trusting others and, therefore, may be unable to form deep, trusting relationships in later years. The ability to bond is considered crucial for the development of a healthy sexuality by the advocates of bonding.

Brazelton (1983) notes there has been a major change in many hospitals toward tieing the family together by giving the newborn child to each parent immediately after birth. Mothers sometimes breast feed the baby while still on the delivery table. "Birthing" rooms are becoming common in hospitals where both parents and often other family members are present and may participate directly in the delivery. Parents who have participated frequently claim that they know and feel the baby is theirs from the moment of birth.

Brazelton (1981) reports on the unmedicated infant at term whose quiet calmness for a considerable period following delivery seems to indicate a seeking. The goal is said to be contact - skin, eye, voice, and breast - with at least one adult human who will then be primary in the child's life. When and if the contact is established and maintained consistently, the baby is free to turn properly egocentric energies toward his or her own development.

Students of Early Childhood Development agree that the quality of early parent-child bonding is crucial, but there is disagreement as to whether infants and children under three can form the necessary attachments if both parents work full-time. However, there is no reason to believe that poor bonding is due only to frequent parental absences. Certainly the quality of a day care center or the personal characteristics of those who do take care of the child is influential. There are many who believe that one of the parents should be in the home full time for the first six months to establish proper bonding. Segal and Segal (1985) contend that the bonding process is not a static one-time event, but a dynamic and continuous relationship over several months. They posit a close and loving bond as being possible even if contact is delayed for various reasons, such as in a case of adoption.

Most writers describe the nature of human sexuality starting with birth, but Calderone (1985, p. 700) believes that the nature of sexuality in the fetal months should be comprehended. She writes; "Testosterone causes the male sex and reproductive organs to begin their development; as early as 17 weeks' gestation, erections of the tiny penis have been noted by ultrasound technology . . ." She adds that there is no reason that the female response system cannot be presumed to function in utero, even though the reproductive system only begins to function years later. The importance of fetal sexuality is to provide the base on which the evolution of children to adolescence is built.

Because babies who are breast fed have a special relationship with their mother, many students of the family consider this to be a positive factor, more significant than bottle feeding, which can be done by anyone. Although it is not feasible for many working mothers to breast feed their babies, some would recommend that it be done once a day or so for a few weeks if possible. (See Figure 1-4) During breast feeding, the child is being held, touched and talked to by the mother, in addition to receiving the best of food. The socialization process is being facilitated through these sensory experiences. The human being lives in a world of sights, sounds, smells, and objects, therefore the infant's experiences during feeding are an integral part of this development.

The many positive aspects of breast feeding should not be taken to mean that the bottle fed baby is seriously deprived. The most important factor is not whether the milk comes from a breast or a bottle but the amount of human contact and loving the infant receives during his feeding. Children need physical contact and most children enjoy being held, touched, played with, caressed, and kissed. They not only need this from parents and other adults but from children at different ages. Toddlers from one to three years of age can often be observed climbing over each other, hugging, kissing, and wrestling. Touching and responding to touch are critical needs in early childhood. They are major ingredients in the full development of sexuality and sensual learning. This can be as effectively accomplished by parents with limited time to spend with their child as by those who devote full time to child-rearing.

Another way the sexuality of a small child develops comes from observing the relationship between his or her parents and those other persons most involved in the rearing process. The child sees whether these adults do or do not enjoy each other, and whether they have respect for each other; they notice the ways in which they express their love, anger, and other emotions, and how they relate to each other physically. Similarly, the interplay among siblings, relatives, and neighbors will be influential for the child in a limited environment. It has consistently been found that children from happy homes and children with a happy

A four year old boy and a six year old girl were discussing their baby brothers. The boy's brother was bottle fed and he had difficulty understanding how the little girl's brother nursed. The girl made this drawing of her mother and explained her mother's breast and nipples and how her baby brother was fed by milk from her mother's body.

Figure 1-4 Baby getting milk

childhood are happier in later years, have happier marriages, and a better relationship with other people.

Maureen

One summer day, eight year old Maureen walked into the kitchen and saw her father standing behind her mother and holding her tightly with his hands cupped around her breasts. The little girl quietly turned and walked out of the kitchen and began to reflect on what she had seen. Her parents often hugged each other, so she decided that her father was holding her mother's breasts as a part of their expression of love for each other. Suddenly she remembered that she had seen her parents do the same thing when she was a little girl and that it made her feel warm and good because Mommy and Daddy loved each other and because she knew they loved her too.

When the first child comes into the life of a married couple, it creates a new and complicated set of relationships in addition to changing the one between the husband and wife. Each additional child also disturbs the existing relations as well as creating new ones between the baby and the others in the family. Adjustments to these new relationships are not easy and friction arises on occasion, so the infant is quickly exposed to negative factors in addition to positive ones of love and affection. For example, the father may experience jealousy and frustration due to the baby's taking possession of his wife's breasts for feeding purposes. The toddler may decide to return to the mother's breast when the baby is observed nursing. Older children may feel less loved due to the heavy demands on time and attention by the newcomer and become resentful because of the rivalry. This competition may also create tensions among the older children themselves as they compete for attention and affection.

Families inevitably develop routines in the various phases of daily life. This includes sitting at the same place in the living room and at the dining room table, going to bed in the same manner at the same time each evening, eating a particular meal every Sunday, and keeping the furniture arranged in a given pattern. A new baby disrupts almost every routine. The need for silence because the baby is sleeping can be an annoyance. The costs of having and rearing an infant are met by reducing expenditures in other areas - food, recreation, clothes, and the like. If the relations among family members is thought of as a distribution of power, a baby forces a redistribution. The resulting struggle for a new position of power can create high tensions at times. Hopefully, the young siblings of the baby learn from all the disruptive factors and gain an increased understanding of the social nature of humans. It must not be forgotten that these dynamics of relationships apply with each additional child, i.e., a family of four is different from a family of five.

A more serious complication brought about by the new baby is the interruption, at least temporarily, in the sexual activity and feelings of the husband and wife. During the post-partum healing period, the mother may have little or no interest in sex. Heavy demands of the infant create fatigue and lack of opportunity for making love. The parents may focus primarily on the requirements of that role and minimize their relations as husband and wife. On occasion, wives come to reject sex because they do not wish to have more children. Without elaborating further on all the possibilities brought about by a new child, it should be obvious that these situations and adjustments will affect relationships with the baby. It is especially important to note that they will cause the infant to experience negative situations due to the tensions present in the family as a whole. In the development of his or her own sexuality, the infant will be scolded, neglected, pinched, and teased, so that in many ways they will sense that life is not all pleasant and easy. On the positive side, the little child will be hugged, kissed, patted, and shown love and affection in many ways. The small child functions in terms of immediacy - delayed gratification is not relevant here - so the happy stimulation from those who care will usually be dominant. The inexperienced infant is influenced by each act and responds primarily to the people that are known - parents, siblings, and those most frequently available. All of this is a part of the preparation for the complex world in which growth will take place. Within limits, some negative experiences for the small child are a valuable part of this development and will contribute to a stronger and healthier sexuality.

TWO DIFFERENT PATHS

In this section of the chapter there are the stories of two children who have experienced very contrasting experiences in the development of their sexuality. One received abuse and neglect while the other received love and guidance. While the future can not be predicted, the opportunities and probabilities of a stable and well-adjusted adolescence and adulthood are certainly not the same for Damon and Jennie. Attitudes toward life, trust in others, and rewarding relationships are important aspects of the development of a healthy sexuality. These two children have quite contrasting situations and consequences even while they are quite young.

Damon

Damon entered kindergarten as a very unhappy

youngster who demanded the undivided attention of all children and adults with whom he came into contact. He hit, kicked, screamed, teased, and tormented the other children. With the teachers, he disobeyed every rule and yelled and demanded they grant his every wish.

Most children tried to avoid him, as they did not enjoy playing with him. He would attempt to bribe some of the others with candy and toys so they would play with him and did have some limited success.

He was very "streetwise" with a vocabulary of slang and four-letter words. Punishment, scolding, and even attempting to talk with him was quite ineffective in stopping these disruptive activities. Damon would say to a little girl, "Pull up your blouse and show me your bra and boobs." He often grabbed at another boy's penis or he would take his pants down and want the other boys to touch him. On one occasion when the teacher, Mr. Morgan, stopped this type of activity, he said to Damon, "That kind of behavior is wrong. Those parts of your body covered by your bathing suit are private and should not be touched by anyone else unless your mother or a doctor has a good reason." Damon replied, "I know but it is fun and it feels good." An hour after this incident, Damon and a little girl were putting their hands down the back of each others' underpants.

Mr. Morgan tried various approaches, including behavior modification, to help Damon. "Time out" was used on occasion whereby the child is removed from the group to gain self-control and reflect on the unacceptable behavior. The method is not designed to be punishment and create a sense of guilt, but to aid the child in learning what is acceptable and what is not. At times, Damon was strongly resistant to "time out." However, the teacher remained firm and continued to work toward Damon's cooperation. This method often helps children achieve emotional and social growth; in Damon's case it was mostly ineffective. When the boy rejoined the group, sometimes at Mr. Morgan's request or perhaps by his own decision, he usually resumed the same behaviors that had disrupted the group previously.

Damon was highly verbal and imparted much information to his teacher and other school personnel about his home environment. Sometimes he gave conflicting information: he said his Daddy lived elsewhere, that he was dead, or that he never had a Daddy. He also talked about his mother's boyfriends and some of the sexual activities that were engaged in. From other sources, it was reported that she was a user of cocaine. On several occasions when she came to pick up Damon, she seemed to be intoxicated.

Several conferences were held with the mother during the school year. At this point, the teacher made a referral of Damon to the school guidance counsellor. The school counselor discussed Damon's abilities and his problems with the mother and made a number of positive suggestions but they appeared to be ineffective. She refused to take the child to a pediatric psychiatrist as recommended by the counselor. Damon gradually gained some acceptance during the year from his peers, but the lack of helpful guidance from his mother and the unstable home life are negative influences in these early years.

Jennie

Three year old Jennie stopped playing with the new doll her father had given her the night before and said to her aunt, "Aunt Sherrie, isn't it time to go home and see my Mommy and baby Alicia? I want to hold the baby. I want to ask Mommy how she was born."

For several months, Jennie and her parents had discussed and made many plans for the coming of the baby. Jennie had helped choose the colors and the equipment for the nursery. She went with her father to buy a crib, and her father let her buy a present for the baby and one for herself. On one occasion she went with her mother to the doctor's office and the doctor let Jennie hear her own heartbeat and that of the baby developing inside her mother's womb.

When the mother and the baby came home, Jennie was waiting with her aunt. Jennie's mother hugged and kissed her and told her to sit beside her so she could see and hold her new sister. This was fun for Jennie but she enjoyed it even more as Alicia grew older and began to respond with smiles and laughter. She was a well-adjusted child who had been well-prepared by her parents for the new baby. Usually the sisters related well to each other in their play and were very physical with a lot of hugging and kissing, and other contacts involving touching. At times, Jennie would become annoyed with her little sister and refuse to play with her. The parents did not interfere because she made no attempt to physically harm the baby. The parents felt that some anger and jealousy are normal behavior in the development of children and that it was desirable for both children, if not carried to extremes. At the same time, the parents exhibited a great love and affection for the two children and for each other and did it quite openly. Jennie and Alicia are learning to relate to people in a most positive manner, one based on love and trust. While negative experiences are sure to happen to them as time goes by, their ability to cope is quite strong because they are secure in their feelings about themselves.

The contrasts between Damon and Jennie are quite substantial in terms of their experiences, their family, and the attitude of others toward them. Damon's sexuality as it is developing is full of unhappiness, rejection, and a continuing uncertainty as to how he will be treated in each situation as it comes along. He lacks the support from others to help meet his problems, and he lacks the confidence in himself to achieve acceptance as he goes along. Jennie, on the other hand, believes the world is a most pleasant place and that everyone is her friend. She has been treated most kindly by others and feels secure in her daily life. There is little reason to think that even when things go wrong, she will not be able to define them as exceptions and continue in a positive vein. Perhaps the most important consideration is the fact that the future as it unfolds will be interpreted in terms of the past, so that a negative happening breeds suspicion of more negativism, and vice versa. It must be assumed that any pattern can be changed and that each child has a chance to get ahead; but, as this book will point out, sexuality is cumulative - happiness contributes to more happiness whereas unhappiness tends to lead in that direction. The importance of exploring the sexual development of the young child is that he has had fewer experiences and thus there is less to undo when he begins to encounter problems that are beyond his grasp.

A WORKING DEFINITION OF SEXUALITY

Sexuality in the broadest sense encompasses an individual's personal growth in all its dimensions including the ways a person relates to others. We are all sexual beings; sexuality is not something we do, but is what we are. We create a sexual identity, male or female, in terms of the behavior which develops as masculine or feminine. Each of us has our own unique sexuality. Physiological, social, cultural, biological, and emotional forces have contributed in a multitude of ways to make us the sexual beings we are. This conditioning, beginning at birth and based on biological and genetic factors, is a continuing process until death.

Sexuality is the term that includes the biological nature of a person, the physical aspects of sex relations, and the many other aspects of sex-linked behavior. The physical aspects are often projected as being dominant by today's mass media, but they are not the essence of sexuality. Most often, they represent a distortion to a large degree inasmuch as sex is centered around the genitalia and sensual responses rather than toward sexual expression involving the personality and relationship with others. The goal in developing human sexuality is much more than the attainment of sexual gratification through the sex act or other kinds of stimulation. The goal is the integration of our conception of ourself, our behavior, our value system, into our interaction with others. When our sexuality is developed in an integrated manner, a meaningful series of relationships with other people during each of the various stages of life become attainable and sustainable.

A child's sex affiliation, biologically speaking, is normally observable at birth. There is present the ability to be stimulated sexually as well as some sexual capabilities. Erections or secretions in the vagina may begin to occur the first few weeks of life (some say earlier). Parents of young children need to recognize the importance of facilitating a sexual identity utilizing these capabilities and the potential which exists. This process, whether carried out wisely or not, begins immediately as infants are assisted in learning who they are, what they are, and what they can and should do in various situations. They also learn that much of this learning will change as they becomes older. Such growth is comparable to the learning of a new language: namely by learning some basics, by interacting with others and emulating them, and by experiencing acceptance and/or rejection at each stage. In the early months and years of life, parents and others involved with the child are the crucial influences in this growth and learning process. Money & Tucker (1975, p. 127) emphasize the early years when they write: "Consistency in the signals a child gets from his two parents as to what behavior is acceptable for each sex is essential to his or her development. Schemes can be modified to some extent throughout life, but the early years are the critical period for developing pride and confidence in one's masculinity or femininity." The characteristics of families and the different ways fathers and mothers contribute to boys and girls is explored in some detail later in the book. Later, persons outside the home, especially those in the educational system, including pre-school programs, become increasingly significant for the child's sexuality.

The primary focus should center on how the child can be helped to develop his sexuality in the most positive manner, not on sex instruction. A young child receives sex information and learns about sexuality from many sources but mostly from the home and play environment. During the stages of growth, the child gradually acquires a sexual identity and learns about human behavior through daily interaction with the "significant others" in his life. These especially important people, along with the social and cultural variations to which one is exposed, may both help and hinder the development of sexuality in a constructive way. Because the effects of sexuality continue throughout life, it is necessary to provide the child with sound guidance and parental understanding during the formative years if there is to be a stable foundation for adulthood. If the influence and guidance of parents, teachers, and the others is positive, earlier learnings will continue to be reinforced.

For a child to develop into a mature adult who can function constructively in society, he or she must feel secure; receive love; have physical and intellectual needs met; and experience the freedom, within limits, to explore the environment. A child needs to be protected from excessive fears, anxieties, and severe frustrations, but if they occur, help must be provided to cope with them. Fears and anxieties may become manifest in nightmares or night terrors. The child requires reassurance and comforting - being held in the parent's arms is often enough - so as to feel that everything is all right. Children respond differently to frustration. One may repeat building a stack of blocks over and over again, another may try twice and walk away, and a third will kick the blocks or begin to cry. The first child needs some instruction, the second should be encouraged to "stick with it" a little longer, and the third may need loving attention directed toward control of emotions in relation to a minor problem. The adage "learn by doing" sometimes needs to be evaluated for a particular child in a particular situation. Sometimes when children fight over a toy, they will ultimately resolve the situation by themselves, but occasionally an adult will need to control the situation. Children need acceptance and understanding as they learn through trial and error to develop a sexual identity and their sexuality in general.

In sum, the basic sexual needs of the infant and pre-school child are met when the parents and teachers openly demonstrate their love and understanding, whether the child exhibits acceptable or unacceptable behavior. Sources of strength obtained early in life enable the child to channel sexual drives appropriately and to attain meaningful relationships with others. The less effective the parent, the more crucial the teacher's role becomes in developing sound human sexuality for the young child.

QUESTIONS FOR DISCUSSION

1. What kinds of problems does inaccurate information create for the sexual development of young children? What about incomplete information? Does poorly presented information, even if correct, create problems? In what way?

2. Compare the relative merits of spontaneous versus planned activities in educating young children about sexuality.

3. What are the possibilities of bonding in cases where a young child is adopted several months after birth? If a young child is in and out of the hospital during the first few years, how might this affect the bonding process?

4. What are some positive and negative aspects of family routines in daily living? What are the consequences when a newborn child joins the family?

5. In a developmental approach, achievements are related to age; how does this apply to the acquiring of a healthy sexuality?

CHAPTER REFERENCES

Brazelton, T. (1981). On becoming a family: the growth of attachment. New York: Dell.

Brazelton, T. (1983). Infants and mothers. (rev. ed.) New York: Delacorte Press.

Calderone, M. (1985). Adolescent sexuality: elements and genesis. Pediatrics, 76; 699-703.

Money, J. & P. Tucker. (1975). Sexual signatures: on being a man or a woman. Boston: Little Brown and Company.

Segal, J. & Z. Segal. (1985). Growing up smart and happy. New York: McGraw Hill.

Whittlestone, W.G. (1989). Background to bonding. Child and Family, 19: 84-97.

CHAPTER II

THE YOUNG CHILD
LEARNS A WAY OF LIFE

A GIANT STEP: LEARNING SEXUALITY IN
THE WORLD OF PRE-SCHOOL

A young child's horizons will broaden considerably when he or she enters a pre-school program and meets a variety of children from other neighborhoods, other religions, other races, and most importantly, with other backgrounds, parental training, and experiences. For the first time, he or she may encounter selfishness or generosity, meanness or kindness, fighting, children with emotional or mental problems, and sharing with others. The child will learn to respond to an adult other than a parent or babysitter who will insist on being obeyed on occasion. Whether the child enters an Infant School, Day Care, Head Start, Nursery, Public or Private Kindergarten, Montessori, or other organized grouping, a new phase in socialization will be encountered.

Youngsters are quite differently prepared to enter a school environment. The child from a large family has been advised about the nature of school by older siblings while an only child has not. A child with a working mother has dealt with persons outside the family in an authoritative position. One person may have been taught to share but another has not. A child such as Damon, discussed earlier, will likely be on the defensive and be aggressive as a protective mechanism, while one like Jennie may not be well prepared for the competition for toys, teachers favors, and especially for "best friends."

In this chapter the emphasis will be primarily on the teacher's role and responsibility in guiding these young children as they enter a new phase in the development of their sexuality. There is more emphasis on

Figure 2-1 *(Photo courtesy of Diane Wilson)*

the kindergarten, because almost all children are exposed to its programs and activities. None of the other young child school situations are as common nor do they affect as many children. It should be noted that the instructors, supervisors, and teachers in these various pre-school programs are prepared in different degrees and in different ways to handle a variety of children and situations. Some programs have professionally trained and certified teachers while some have interested and willing, but generally untrained personnel. In general, the better prepared the teacher, the better the environment for the child, but there are also less tangible factors of importance. Sometimes a person will be attracted to another person without a clear idea as to why. It may be reciprocated by the other person or it may not. A teacher and a child may find themselves in the same situation and it will affect their relationship. A child who truly responds to the teacher is more receptive to the ideas and information offered than if he or she does not feel comfortable. When a young person feels unloved or unwanted, whether at home or in the pre-school system, it affects the interpretation of all that happens to him or her. It is easier to react positively to the bright child, the obedient one, and the "lovable" little boy or girl than it is to the aggressive or uncooperative child. To some extent, a sense of love and caring will compensate for other problems, but not entirely. The teacher who is truly professional should be able to minimize personal feelings, but total concealment is extremely difficult.

The world of the nursery or day care is the first experience outside the home and away from the parents for many young children. Other adults, other children, and new ideas and materials will be introduced. Trips to interesting places will open children's eyes to new things. Resource people invited into the program will tell them about persons, places, and things of which they were unaware. Most of all, the child becomes increasingly involved in relationships and personalities. The teacher or supervisor is the catalyst in this system and the degree of effectiveness or ineffectiveness plays a most important part in the sound development of the young child's sexuality.

LEARNING TO RELATE TO OTHERS

Behavioral theorists maintain that individuals must develop the ability to establish meaningful relationships during childhood if they are to function as sexually mature persons during their adolescence and adult years. During the pre-school years, the foundation for later maturity is laid through the experiences necessary for deep associations with others through interaction with family members, peers, and "significant others" encountered in daily living.

In his discussion of human sexuality as the underlying basis of one human's need for relationships with others, Armin Grams (1970) stresses the nature of human development that result in each infant and young child having basic needs fulfilled by others. From this relationship, the strong drive for communion with others is learned. Grams believes that to be able to establish relationships with others, the following capabilities must be developed: the capacity for intimacy with others, competency through learning both facts and skills, receptiveness to others including our need to give as well as to receive love, and faithfulness and trust in our relationships with others. Social scientists generally agree that both physical and psychological nearness are required and develop early in infancy. As our sexuality grows, it may both contribute to these needs and interfere with them.

Sexuality, thus defined, is necessarily a vital component in the socialization process. The teacher plays a critical role when she assists the child in learning to interact with others; to acquire knowledge and attitudes about the continually developing sexual identity; and to have experiences that aid ego-development. A child requires support from others in order to keep the ego intact under conditions of stress. When children are ignored, or think they are, the immediate reaction may well be that one is not loved or wanted because one is bad.

A child who faces a crisis with a healthy ego is likely to need less help than one who has little regard for herself or himself. Those children in crisis situations who have damaged egos or a feeling of rejection for some reason, need to be helped to develop a sense of belonging to a group. Children need guidance in learning to experience love, to appreciate their strengths, to correct their liabilities when possible, and to accept those which they cannot change. A structured play environment is designed to give each child repeated opportunities to achieve success and honest recognition as an individual.

Kathryn D'Evelyn (1970), in her booklet Developing Mentally Healthy Children, points out that it is the teacher's responsibility to make each child feel important and to gain positive feelings about himself or herself. She adds that the school has a major role in aiding ego development in the young child because ego development and learning are very closely related. Studies seem to indicate that, regardless of socio-economic or racial background, the earlier a child has positive experiences that contribute to strong ego development, the better it is for the child. It may be that it is too late to build a strong ego by the time a child reaches kindergarten.

Jack

An experienced kindergarten teacher always made a point of telling her student teachers that every child has many assets and that she had yet to find a child to whom she could not give praise and recognition. Then she encountered Jack. For several weeks she found nothing in Jack's behavior or appearance about which she could honestly offer approval. His negative behavior caused his peers to reject him and made it almost impossible for him to be integrated into classroom activities. One day the teacher noticed Jack imitating Elvis Presley. She quickly congratulated him on his excellent imitation and strong sense of rhythm. She created additional opportunities for him to display his talents to the other children. For several days there were lots of "Elvis Presleys" in the class but none were as good as Jack. Gradually other incidents occurred which permitted her to offer Jack some form of recognition. While he was not yet fully accepted by the group, he slowly began to modify his negative behavior. As he became more accepting of himself and others, he became less isolated and appeared to be a happier child. A stronger ego permitted him to lower his defenses and participate in the group with a sense of belonging.

WHY YOUNG CHILDREN HAVE DIFFICULTIES RELATING TO PEOPLE

One of the major reasons children have difficulty in relating to other people is that they do not feel loved or wanted. A sense of belonging to parents, or to others who care for him or her, enables the child to feel important about himself or herself. When this occurs, he or she is able to associate with others as an equal because of a sense of security and a feeling of worth. On the other hand, it is true that some children do not feel loved or wanted because they aren't. They may be rejected by one or both parents. A child can also feel rejected in foster homes or institutions. The child may be loved and wanted but not realize it because he or she doesn't recognize the signs of caring from the parents or others who are not very demonstrative. The important thing is that unless children believe they are loved, they will be unhappy and troubled.

Some parents with exceptional children, those with with physical or mental handicaps, are unable to communicate the extent of their concern to the child. Often there are ambivalent feelings about the child or guilt feelings about the existence of the handicap and a sense of responsibility. Many handicapped children exhibit behavior that is difficult for parents to understand and cope with. This is especially true of neurologically-impaired children. Many children with severe mental or physical handicaps also place heavy physical, emotional, and financial demands upon the parents. Such problems added to any guilt feelings make it difficult for parents and other people to relate to the children freely and easily.

The kindergarten teacher or other pre-school person may be in a position to help parents communicate their love to their children more effectively. Such persons may be the first to identify a problem, or to interpret its importance for the development of the child. After identifying the problem, they may be able to aid the parents in acquiring more adequate knowledge and understanding of the handicapped child's behavior and how to better meet the various needs. Given this assistance, parents are in a position to express their affection and love more easily.

On the other hand, some parents with exceptional children need guidance in order to not show excessive love or place unnecessary restrictions on their children, thus preventing them from developing their potential freely and acquiring the self-confidence that should go with such achievements. These parents need guidance in recognizing and accepting the need to treat their children as normal (allowing for the limitations established by the nature of the handicap) and to build the child's sexuality on that basis. Exceptional children do not necessarily feel unloved, but those who DO need a great deal of help from the teachers. Every child in the pre-school environment should feel that the teacher accepts him or her. It is with this belief that the teacher can develop the positive steps to help the child.

Todd

Todd was an exceptional child who needed no special help when he entered school. He had parents with sufficient emotional stability and educational background to recognize early that Todd had problems. They also had the financial resources to provide the professional help while he was quite young. The kindergarten teacher was highly skilled and fully familiar with the behavioral characteristics of exceptional children so she often was the first to recognize the children's needs. After working with Todd and observing him, she found him extremely intelligent and quite mature in his social, emotional and physical growth. (See Figure 2-2)

In the classroom, Todd contributed to the learning activities quite successfully, drawing on a wide background of experiences. Unaided, he wrote and illustrated a story about the incubator in the kindergarten room. While his story had no punctuation marks, the words were spelled correctly because he asked the teacher or looked for the written word on charts in the room. Todd was also a strong leader in many of the dramatic play activities. When not leading, he was always cooperative and helpful when playing with other children.

In late spring, Todd took a Readiness Test. He scored in the ninety-ninth percentile in his overall readiness score. Because of his abilities, maturity, and his high score on this test, the parents and teacher thought that a psychological study should be done to determine the proper grade placement for the next school year. The study revealed that Todd's mental age as measured on the Wechsler Intelligence Scale was nine years, seven months in contrast to his chronological age of six years, eight months. Evaluation of his academic achievement revealed that his reading, including comprehension, was

Todd's self-portrait was to be included with his first report card. The drawing reflects his social and emotional maturity. There is fine detail on the clothing and his body is well proportioned. He included all of the body parts that are visible wearing clothes. Also, he has all the features on the head except the ears.

Figure 2-2 Todd's self-portrait

at fourth grade level, spelling at third grade level and arithmetic at beginning second grade. The psychologist stated that Todd appeared to be extremely mature for his age and was emotionally stable.

Todd's home environment contained many positive factors. He came from a home where his parents, both professional people with several graduate degrees, placed a high value on learning. Todd had a good relationship with his parents and siblings, and his behavior indicated that he had received love, security, and good guidance from his parents.

Not until near the end of the school year did Todd's parents reveal to the teacher that they had taken him at age two to a pediatric neurologist who put him on drug therapy. The mother said she became concerned because Todd threw extreme temper tantrums, banged his head on the floor repeatedly, and became rigid. At the mother's insistence, and over the father's protest, the family doctor arranged for Todd to see a specialist.

The neurologist's diagnosis was that the boy had some minimal neurological impairment, but with his other capabilities and proper guidance he could be helped. Todd was placed on drug therapy and his parents were advised on how to teach him to cope with his tensions and frustrations. One method was to remove him from a tension producing situation until he could calmly return to it. By the time he entered kindergarten, Todd could do this on his own. He never once cried or lost control unless he was physically injured.

Todd is an excellent example of a child with a healthy environment for sexual development. His problem was identified early, he received proper professional care and good parental guidance during his childhood. If Todd had entered school with his problems undiagnosed and/or untreated, even with extra love and understanding and a great deal of ego-reinforcement, the teacher would have had a difficult time in helping him to adjust to the new and demanding environment. His progress through the educational system would have been a difficult one because of rejection by others when he displayed his temper and other extreme behavior.

Janie

Some children who have no apparent problems enter

kindergarten and display no interest in interacting with their peers or establishing any relationships with anyone. If a child has been in a pre-school program at an earlier age, this is likely to be resolved as in the case of Janie. When she was four years old, she was entered in a nursery school where she never uttered a word to her teacher or the other children for several weeks. Occasionally she entered into dramatic play but mostly she just sat and watched. When the teacher discussed Janie's behavior with her parents, they said that at home she had no speech problems but talked freely about school. Both parents were as puzzled as the teacher about the little girl's silence. The teacher was able to involve her in dramatic play activities in small groups but was unsuccessful in getting her to talk.

Janie's behavior continued in this manner for almost four weeks until one day the teacher brought a land turtle into the classroom. All the children spent the first day making a home in a box for their new pet. Janie helped make the home and she spent the entire next day by the turtle. On the third day, she began talking to the turtle and then to the children about the turtle. From that point on she began to interact with all the children and talked freely. Being silent for so long a period is rather unusual but does not represent a major problem. Janie needed time to adjust to the new environment before she could begin to relate to the other children and the teacher. This is a major value of the nursery, day care, or kindergarten setting, as they are child-centered environments with equipment and learning experiences that promote language development and social interaction.

Non-verbal interaction is important for a young child's play, but the child uses verbal skills increasingly as maturing occurs and is able to relate more with others. However, highly verbal children can encounter difficulty in interaction with other children if they are immature in other areas.

Bruce

Bruce was reared in his grandparent's home where he and his parents lived while they attended graduate school. Bruce had little opportunity to share playthings or experiences with other children, and his grandparents responded to every whim of this child. A psychological study on Bruce revealed that when he was five years and three months of age, his mental age was almost eight, but his emotional age was only three and one half. He related well to adults in the school environment only if the other children did not prevent him from receiving their exclusive attention. With children, he had greater difficulty as they considered him thoughtless and selfish. He was usually very aggressive, and demanded that they obey his every wish. When the children refused, he would cry, fight with them, and become very angry and frustrated. From the guidance by the teacher and the negative reactions of the other children, Bruce gradually learned to accept the fact that other children had the same desires, and also the same rights to satisfy them, as he did. The more mature youngsters in the group helped him learn to modify his behavior and he gradually learned to cooperate and share with the others.

His concerned parents were receptive to suggestions from the teacher as to how they could help Bruce mature in his emotional and social development. They moved into their own home and the mother restricted her graduate work to evening classes when the father could be home. The father spent more time with Bruce in the evening, and the mother took in another five-year old child to care for during the day. The teacher taught Bruce to modify his unacceptable behavior with the other children, and was able to give him praise and recognition when he used his assets and capabilities constructively in the group. At times she let Bruce experience some conflict with and rejection from the other children, yet she also had to protect him when he could not handle the situation. He gradually began to assume responsibility and be less demanding of his peers, and by the end of the school year he was relating very well with his classmates. While Bruce's problem was primarily due to a combination of poor guidance in the home and the lack of opportunity to interact with other children, it does illustrate two important points about the school's role. First, a five year old can be guided into caring about, respecting, and adjusting successfully with his or her peers. Second, by accentuating the positive aspects of the child's abilities and behaviors and helping eliminate many of the negative actions, much can be done to help young children to succeed in their relationships with their peers.

The importance of helping young people learn to achieve a healthy sexuality in order to establish good relationships with others cannot be overemphasized. From early childhood and throughout their lifetime, human beings strive to overcome their feelings of loneliness and isolation. The intensive dependency of the infant and young child causes him to learn the strong drive for a communion with other people. Most of us are afraid of social isolation so the solitary cell on death row is a more severe penalty than death for many. It is through struggling with our "aloneness," that we strive to belong, to find ourselves, and to gain recognition and appreciation through our involvement with others.

The young child seeks to meet this basic need by wanting to be with others. This is how children learn about themselves and others. He or she may or may not recognize this fear of being alone. He or she may or may not express themselves verbally or behaviorally by showing a fear of the dark, or of new or strange situations. The trauma of separation from mother that some children experience when they first enter school may be a manifestation of this fear. Also young children frequently express their fear of social isolation from their peers. A pre-school teacher is fully aware of a child's fear, anger, and frustration when peers say they dislike him or her or do not want to play with such a child.

Teachers also encounter children who are angry with themselves, their parents, and any other people they encounter. They have already learned to distrust everyone, and the teacher can do little to help these children until they become less angry with themselves. The first step for the teacher is to establish a plan that will help a child of this type to be trustful. From this starting point he or she then can take positive steps to help children become less angry with themselves and others. Guidance, with love, is especially crucial for these children, as they have a desperate need to be accepted by their teachers and peers, even though their behavior may not show it.

The aggressive child is rejected by most peers because of the behavior that is directed toward them. Sometimes the child does this because he or she has been reared in an environment where there was little guidance and thus has experienced few, if any, restrictions. Such a child has not been taught "the rules of the game," and therefore is at a disadvantage when he or she comes in contact with others outside the home. The child has to be helped to learn what the rules are, why they exist, and how to change aggressive behavior into more acceptable ways of interacting with others. An environment that offers children constructive ways of channeling their aggressive behavior is a necessary part of their socialization.

Inasmuch as each child is unique, the teacher will have to seek the reasons why anyone is having difficulty relating to others. D'Evelyn (1970) believes that an experienced teacher should not find it difficult to make each child believe that he or she is an important member of the group. The types of children that are most likely to encounter difficulty are (1) the child who appears to be detached but actually is protecting himself against the demands of life in general and school in particular, (2) the child who has not learned to share or observe the "rules of the game" when participating with others, and (3) the neurologically-impaired or mentally-ill child who cannot control his or her feelings or behaviors in many situations. It is very difficult to integrate these three types into a class but it always necessary for the teacher to attempt to do so and especially to work with the parents in bringing about the best adjustment possible.

It is of utmost importance to help the young child to like himself or herself and others.   While lacking the maturity or intellectual development to achieve a deep relationship, the foundation begins in the pre-school period when the child interacts with family members, peers, and "significant others," the people that are encountered most in daily living. Without the benefit of such associations, a person can not escape loneliness nor achieve the full potentiality of sexuality. By relating to and interacting with others, young children satisfy the need to feel they are not alone, learns about themselves and others, begins to develop understanding of the appropriate sex role, and learns to accept membership in his or her own sex.

Figure 2-3 *(Photo courtesy of Diane Wilson)*

CURIOSITY: ACQUIRING FACTUAL KNOWLEDGE, POSITIVE ATTITUDES, AND ACCEPTABLE BEHAVIOR

Young children discuss with each other and with their teachers a wide variety of subjects, including sexual matters. They ask many questions, such as: "Did I really grow in Mother's stomach?" "Does a baby eat while he is in his mother's stomach?" "Why didn't I hatch from an egg like chickens do?" While the questions are varied, they are usually not complex and require only elementary and honest answers. In their uncomplicated mode of thinking, most children accept the process of birth as matter-of-factly as they accept the landing of our astronauts on the moon. While they are interested and have some knowledge, they lack the maturity to fully understand our space accomplishments. This is also true of the young child's interest in reproduction, but young children are curious about their bodies and the elementary aspects of reproduction. They are very interested in where babies come from and how they are born. It is only logical that they should be curious about such matters, because a new baby in their home or a friend's home is a big event. Their interest in the birth process will be obvious to the pre-school teacher if the children are in a learning environment where they feel free to discuss anything they wish without fear of censure or disapproval.

After the nationally-broadcast television special, "How Life Begins," the teacher, Miss Evans, who had not seen the program, initiated a discussion about sea horses. She told the children that the male sea horse is unique, because the mothers deposit the eggs in his pouch, where he carries them until they hatch. Some children said they had seen that on television the night before. The teacher encouraged those who had seen the program to describe it. This prompted the children to explain to her and each other what they had seen about the birth processes of animals and humans. One child said, "I could not understand why the baby was muddy when he came out of his mother's body." Another child answered, "We have color television and I could see that the baby was not muddy but had some blood on it. My mother said that some babies are like that when they are born." The teacher participated by being a good listener and keeping the dialogue going with questions and occasional comments. The discussion lasted about fifteen minutes with most of the children responding to Miss Evan's attempts to help them understand the general significance of birth.

John

Most unplanned discussions will not have the depth or verbal range that evolved from this television program and many will be more casual and rambling. Such discussions probably will be like the teacher's conversation with John, who lived on a farm and had many opportunities to observe and care for animals. One day he stopped building his block construction to say to Mrs. Curtis, his teacher, "I saw the veterinarian help our cow have her calf last night." The teacher listened while John gave a detailed account of how the doctor pulled the calf out of the cow's body. She then said to John, "I also witnessed this event when I was a child." adding however, that most animals have their babies without any help from human beings. Another little boy who had listened to the discussion said, "I understand how babies grow inside their mother's bodies and that they come out, but I can't figure out how the mother helps them come out." The teacher replied that the mother used her muscles to help the baby come out. John snapped his fingers and said, "I should have thought of that myself." He added, "It makes sense to me because I use my muscles sometimes when I have a bowel movement." The teacher did not tell John and the others that her own mother had tried to keep her from seeing the birth of the calf. Nor did she tell anyone that she had been afraid to describe the event at the time because she felt guilty. John and the others were discussing the event freely and thoughtfully. Some county fairs have birthing barns today where the visitors can see births almost every hour on the hour.

It is not necessary for teachers to rely exclusively upon unplanned classroom experiences because they can plan effectively for the discussions of sexual behavior and control the direction. Resource people, the children's pets, and audio-visual materials are available as aids in structuring appropriate learning activities. As a planned experience, the teacher may obtain a family of animals who can live in the classroom for a while. A pair of guinea pigs and the resultant offspring will contribute to an understanding of the basic concepts of reproduction. While it may be argued that there are significant differences between animals and human beings, there are also similarities and the child can be encouraged to focus on these while retaining an awareness of the differences. Through the experiences resulting from observing and caring for pets, a child can learn the following about reproduction: a male and female are necessary for reproduction to occur; the young are born alive; and the mother gives birth to, and usually cares for and feeds the young babies.

The most positive aspect of unplanned experiences is that the children do not feel manipulated and the spontaneity makes the young people more receptive. They ask more questions and discuss their experiences more freely. A good approach for the teacher when the child asks a question is to explore the child's thoughts about the answer to his or her own question. This provides an opportunity to explore ideas as the child may already know the answer to his or her own question. It also prevents the teacher from misinterpreting the question and confusing children with an answer that makes no sense to them.

Brad

Several children were having a discussion while playing in a play house. Brad was arguing with the others that he did not grow inside his mother's body but was dropped from the sky to the hospital where his parents went to get him. The children asked the teacher to settle the issue. She confirmed that Brad and the others did grow inside the mother's body and that the mother went to the hospital for the actual birth. She suggested that they sit down and talk together. Brad asked, "How does a baby get into a mother's body?" The teacher explained that babies begin growing from a tiny egg and continue developing until they are ready to be born. She reminded them of their recent classroom experiences with an incubator and how the baby chickens grew inside the shell. Brad then asked, "Are dog and cat babies born like people or do they hatch from eggs?" After being urged to think about it, the children received an answer and returned to their play.

Later Brad came to the teacher with the question, "Does the mother go to the hospital to be cut open so the baby can get out?" The teacher answered that usually the mother uses certain muscles to push the baby out. She added that sometimes it is necessary to have the baby by an operation and this is called a Caesarian birth. Brad then asked why dogs and cats don't go to the hospital like people do, and the teacher replied that not all people do but it is a good idea because the mother and baby get good care. When asked if he understood, Brad said, "Yes, I guess so. The baby comes out where your bowels move." It was explained that there is a special opening called the vagina but that men do not have it. Brad replied that his father had told him that men couldn't have babies but that he had a penis which girls do not have.

After school, the teacher called the mother to relate the incident and to explain that under the circumstances she had to give some pretty straightforward answers. The mother said that Brad had never asked her any questions and she had never told him anything. She added that she had been waiting until he asked her but since he had asked the teacher first, she was glad that the teacher had answered his questions.

The amount and type of sex information a child receives at home is not usually known to the teacher but she can quickly identify the child who has gotten no or incorrect information. The teacher must be aware, however, that children will have varying needs and different levels of readiness for learning and also come from quite divergent life styles. Many students have parents who are quite secure in their own sexuality, have established a secure emotional environment, and provided adequate sex instruction in the home. Other children have been told a number of things but their home environment is such that this knowledge has a negative impact upon the child's developing sexuality. Still others may come from a home where the environment is conducive to learning but no information about sex and human relationships has been given. Unfortunately, there are some young persons who come from environments in which negative factors hinder their emotional development and learning and who have been given little or no accurate information. Children who have received large doses of incorrect information will have to unlearn it sooner or later, often with unpleasant consequences for their sexuality.

Teachers who are already involved in a planned sex education program as a regular part of their school's curriculum may be provided with a specific outline to follow or they work from only a set of objectives. Some sex education programs currently begin at the preschool level, and some pilot programs are restricted to such programs. This book is not designed to evaluate such programs. Nevertheless, the more knowledgeable teachers are about young children's sexuality development, the more effective they will be in any program. (See Figure 2-4)

The problems many communities have had with the concept of sex education in the schools have caused teachers and administrators to be concerned about providing sex information to the young child. A common parental objection to sex education in the schools is that the parents should be responsible for providing this information to their child. This is less likely to be a problem in programs for young children because they are less formal and many situations are spontaneous, but

MoMMe PreGNant

A six year old boy was writing a letter to his grandfather. When his mother asked if he needed help, he replied "no". His mother, eight months pregnant, mailed this illustrated letter to his grandfather without adding any comments.

Figure 2-4 Mommy pregnant

problems do occur. The teacher's responsibility in such instances is to be alert to the possibility of a problem and to respect the parents' wishes. The majority of parents who do not answer their children's questions about sexual considerations are appreciative rather than resentful when the teacher takes this role. In some cases, the teacher will provide a partial answer and recommend that the child pursue the matter at home. Often the parent will suggest that the child take up his questions with his teacher.

Some public and private school systems have regulations that prohibit teachers from imparting any sex instruction to children, including those in a pre-school program. Some systems permit sex instruction only if it is in the stated curriculum and written permission is obtained from the parents. It is the responsibility of a teacher to know and abide by the rules and regulations in each particular situation. Without guidelines or restrictions, teachers must use their own judgment in responding to questions and situations, making allowances for the nature of the opportunity and the maturity of the children.

Another complication of the situation appears when a teacher experiences discomfort or uneasiness even when dealing with the most elementary questions about sex. For some this concern is present only if other adults are around. The wisest thing for such a teacher to do under the circumstances is to acknowledge the fact that she or he cannot discuss sexual matters without embarrassment and not attempt to answer the child at that time. However a capable teacher should be able to redirect the child's questions or attention as well as behavior, and sometimes this can be done without the child realizing what has occurred. Young children are quite perceptive and if they become aware of the teachers uneasiness or diverting tactics, it could create some negative influences in the child's own development.

One difficult question that might arise for a teacher of pre-school children is "How does the father's sperm get into the mother and produce the baby?" Regardless of the specific form a question in this area may take, some responses will require a continuing series of answers, while others will be too simplistic or too complex to permit any further discussion. The young child who says he or she knows that the mother has an egg in her body and the father has sperm cells, does not necessarily grasp any relationship between the two facts.

Debbie

When Debbie asks her teacher a question about how reproduction takes place, the following are four possible approaches by different teachers:

Teacher A, embarrassed, tells Debbie that only her mother can answer this question and immediately changes the subject. She avoids the issue, closes the door to further communication, and causes Debbie to wonder why she acted so strange.

Teacher B first tries to avoid the issue by telling Debbie that she is far too young to understand. When the girl persists, the teacher says that Mommy and Daddy hold each other close in their arms and this gives the mother the sperm cell. This doesn't mean much to Debbie or satisfy her but she doesn't know other questions to ask.

Teacher C starts by asking Debbie to explain how she thinks her mother gets the sperm cell. Debbie may have picked up some fairly accurate information or she may have some completely wrong ideas gotten from her peers or some older children. When the teacher realizes that Debbie does not know, she tells the girl that the sperm cell, or semen, comes from the father's penis. The penis is inserted into the mother's birth canal or vagina. The teacher then explains that when the sperm comes into contact with the egg cell, a baby starts to grow and continues growing until it is ready to be born.

Teacher D gives the same answer to Debbie, adding that this is called "making love." She says that married people do it because it makes them feel good and shows their love for each other. The teacher then commented that some people make love when they are not married. She had no ready answer when Debbie asked, "Why do people make love when they are not married?" Teacher D said that she can't really answer that question but she doesn't think its a good idea because a baby born to an unmarried woman would not have a father to take care of him or her.

All four teachers reacted to this most difficult question, but only two provided answers. Teacher C used the most effective approach because she first checked the child's knowledge and attitudes and then answered the question honestly and directly. Teacher D provided more information than was necessary to answer the question and then introduced some unnecessary ideas for the child to reflect on without the maturity to understand.

It is appropriate to answer a child's questions at the time it is asked, but it is unwise to answer with details beyond the child's level of understanding. It is important to be frank but strictly to the point and limited to the topic of the moment. Children are sexual beings as are all of us, they are curious, and they have a right to answers to their questions.

An important part of a pre-school teacher's responsibility includes giving a child information and helping him or her to develop positive attitudes while learning. Teachers should be as helpful in areas of sexuality as in specialized topics such as art and music. Teachers who feel uncomfortable when questions involving sex information come up should work very hard to overcome such feelings. One key is to learn the correct terminology and using it when talking with the child. The teacher needs to be at ease when using such words as: pregnancy, uterus, birth canal, vagina, penis, anus, breasts, nipples, and testicles. Other words may come up in discussions but it is not usually necessary to correct the child unless street language or vulgarities are being used. It is important that the proper terms be used and that the child be encouraged to add them to his vocabulary.

Children sometimes discuss intimate and personal matters with their teachers. This may result in embarrassment and concern for the parents even though the child does it in total innocence. One little girl related to her teacher in considerable detail the facts about her father's vasectomy and why he had the operation. The child did not use the term "vasectomy" and there was no reason for the teacher to correct her. Professional ethics require that the teacher not betray this trust by revealing such information to anyone, including other teachers or even the child's parents, without a defensible reason.

In essence, the teacher's role is to allow any discussion of sexual matters that: fits into the educational process; provides an environment where children feel free to ask questions or discuss topics that interest them; earns the trust of the children by being fair and honest with them; and establishes rapport with open lines of communication where children know they will be listened to and their questions will be answered honestly at the time they are asked. It is not only the "what" but the "how" that is important in imparting sex information to the young child.

TEACHERS AND PARENTS WORKING TOGETHER

"Teachers and Parents as Partners" is a common theme among educators today, and there are many advantages for the child when his parents and teachers have rapport and work together. This approach has great impact at the pre-school level, where it can be initiated when parents enroll their child in school. Time is usually allotted for the teacher to meet and talk with the child and parents, whether the educational setting be nursery, day care center, kindergarten, Head Start, or other federally supported programs. Conferences can be arranged at any time during the year to pursue situations as they develop.

During the first encounter the child will be evaluating the teacher as they talk and exploring the physical environment. The teacher will be evaluating the child and both parents and simultaneously will be giving the parents an opportunity to impart information about their child. The parents will be evaluating the teacher's capabilities and develop expectations about the acceptance, respect, and guidance their child will receive while under his or her care.

The major responsibility for establishing rapport is the teacher's. This is not easy with some parents for a variety of reasons. Some parents feel insecure and inadequate as parents and see their child's teacher as a threat, since the teacher may be the first to recognize they feel inferior as parents. Others may experience real unhappiness or conflict because they fear an outsider may jeopardize their relationship with their child. Young children often tell their teacher that they love her or him more than "Mommy," and although the teacher knows that many children make this remark, a parent may be upset. Some parents suffer real trauma when their child enters school, especially those parents who are so overly protective that they think no one else can care for their child as they do. Although the responsibility for establishing rapport and good communication rests primarily with the teacher, and although some parents will be rather distant, most parents will make real contributions to a good relationship. The majority of parents are eager for their child to enter school and some will state quite frankly that they are happy to have someone else assist them with the twenty-four hour a day responsibility they had before the child entered school.

Although parents of the pre-school child are usually eager for guidance and help with their child, they are nonetheless somewhat reluctant to seek aid when concern arises over some areas of their child's development or behavioral problems. They may attempt to secure assistance from their child's teacher, their physician, or other specialists who may be available to them. This is true for parents of nursery, kindergarten, day care, pre-kindergarten, and Head Start children, as the basic concerns are the same for parents of all socio-economic levels. Parents in a lower socio-economic level, however, may not have access to the specialists and to the literature that is available to aid parents (Morgan, 1989).

A legitimate question is, "Can and should teachers give guidance to parents who are concerned about their young child's sexuality?" The answer is yes. Teachers should offer guidance to the child in the school environment and be available to parents if the need arises. They have their educational and experiential background to aid them, and also the advantage of being more objective than the parents about their child's behavior. They may be the only professional available to some parents. Those who seek out other professionals still may want to confer with them for the purpose of gaining information as well as seeking guidance. In any case, the more knowledgeable the teacher, the better for all concerned.

If the teacher does feel uninformed, he or she should seek insight and knowledge about pre-school sexuality through reading, talking to educational and medical specialists, and attending college courses and workshops. Specialists such as psychologists are usually available for consultation regardless of the kind of school setting. Some colleges and universities are now offering workshops, graduate and undergraduate courses, and seminars dealing with human sexuality. These courses are usually designed to educate the student in all areas of human sexuality, and many have as their major focus sex education in the public schools. Public and university libraries have excellent resource materials on human sexuality, including good audio-visual materials. There is a limited amount, however, written specifically about the infant's and young child's sexuality, and the kind of guidance that should be given. A teacher of young children may find it necessary to research the areas of interest or concern and integrate the findings with knowledge from an educational orientation.

As the teacher works with parents, he or she will encounter a wide variety of problems related to pre-school sexuality. These problems may be psychological difficulties or physiological defects in the child, or they may be problems only in the eyes of the parents. The latter situation arises when parents do not understand that the behavior is a normal phase of the child's developing sexuality. In any type of problem the parents may seek guidance or the teacher may have to take the initiative. Some parents will be aware that a problem or potential problem exists but some will not. It is possible that they already have the help they need from other sources; in other cases, the teacher is the only person available to turn to for help with their child.

Keith

Keith's mother asked his kindergarten teacher to help her with a difficult problem. She told the teacher that she did not know how to tell Keith how babies are born, so she told him she had found him behind a rock. This deception was compounded because he did not know he was adopted, and now his biological mother was living next door. Keith's adoptive mother explained that her niece, Keith's biological mother, had called her at the time of his birth and said she did not want the child but would give him to the aunt if she would pay the hospital bill. The aunt did so and later adopted Keith, through the court.

The problem had now become acute because Keith's half brothers were saying to him, "Your mother is not your mother - our mother is your mother." She asked the teacher to tell the little boy how babies are born and to explain his adoption to him. The teacher said she thought it would be better for him to learn this from his mother, who could start by simply saying that a baby grows inside his mother's uterus until it is time to be born. The teacher added that if Keith asked her in school, she would give him a simple, honest answer, but she would suggest that he discuss it with his mother first.

Because of the complexity of the problem, the teacher suggested a three-way conference with the school psychologist. The mother agreed. At the meeting, the psychologist recommended that the mother be the one to tell Keith how babies are born and to tell him, if he asked, that he was adopted. The psychologist added that he did not think it wise to tell Keith who his biological mother was at this early age, but she should continue to stress how much she loved and wanted him.

The teacher commented that from her observations, Keith appeared to be a happy and secure child who reflected a home environment of love and security. When the mother left, she said she appreciated the help and would do as they suggested. She added that the father loved Keith but that he told her that it was the mother's responsibility to tell the boy what he should know.

A little later, Keith approached his teacher and said, "My mother said you would tell me how babies are born, and what adopted means because I am adopted." The teacher was startled but a visitor who overheard the question said the teacher gave good answers and handled the situation quite well, despite having no warning it was coming. The teacher subsequently called the mother and explained what had happened. The mother said she was most appreciative but that she had not suggested that Keith ask his teacher. Keith is now in junior high school, and each year at Christmas and Valentine's Day, the teacher receives a small gift, always signed, "Love, Keith." She doesn't know whether Keith is expressing his love for

someone who is still a very "significant other" in his life
or the mother indicating her gratitude for the help she
received when she had no one else to turn to.

It is not unusual for parents to be concerned about some aspect of
their child's sexuality and yet, because of the nature of the problem, are
unable to discuss it. If they are reasonably well-informed about child
development, and able to identify the nature of problems that exist,
parents are likely to contact their family doctor or pediatrician first.
While some physicians are primarily interested in the child's physical
development rather than the total development, many doctors do play a
vital role in helping parents understand their child's sexuality in the
broadest sense. If there are medical or physiological problems at birth,
doctors are the primary source of information for the parents. They may
refer the parents to other professionals for psychological problems.
Teachers are not necessarily involved in these areas although it may be
necessary for them to be advised about the recommendations and
treatments prescribed.

It is through conferences with parents that teachers can give the most
help. A teacher may recommend conferences with a wide variety of
professionals to deal with a child's needs but personalized guidance
cannot and should not be given to parents in a group meeting. The pre-
school teacher has a degree of intimacy with the children that must be
respected and protected at all costs.

Whether working with parents individually or in groups, a pre-
school teacher must recognize and respect the fact that many parents do
not have comparable knowledge or experience. A teacher who is quite
comfortable discussing sexual matters and using correct terminology
must be aware that many parents are not at ease hearing such terms, or
they may not even understand those terms. The best approach for the
teacher when discussing sensitive matters is to watch for and use cues
from the parents.

There are several areas for concern when teachers attempt to help
parents with problems involving their pre-school children. First, while
teachers are professionals in their own right, they are trained as
educators and not as medical specialists or psychologists. They do not
have the qualifications for intensive family counselling. Teachers
should be able to cope with many problems in the area of the pre-school
child's sexuality but must also recognize that some situations are outside
their areas of expertise. These should be referred to the appropriate
resources in the community, including mental health associations,
psychologists, psychiatrists, neurological pediatricians, and many of
the United Way agencies.

A second concern arises from the pre-school child's unique relationship with the teacher. Beyond the parents and close relatives, the teacher is often the most "significant other" in the child's life. The young child can form very strong attachments to these teachers. The unique environment in the pre-school setting, plus the responsiveness of the child, contribute to a very close relationship in a great many cases. These factors may interfere with the teacher's need to stay objective about the child while working with the parents. It is not uncommon for professionals in any discipline who work with children to over identify with those children and then find it difficult to maintain a clinically sound relationship with the parent. To be effective in working with the parents, the teacher must be alert to these dangers and at the same time, to have some understanding and appreciation of the parent's role.

Jill

It was difficult for Miss Ames to remain calm and not display anger when she went into the conference with Jill's parents. Jill demanded constant attention from her teacher, often saying, "I want you to love me because my Mommy doesn't."

Miss Ames had never been able to arrange a conference before because Jill's mother always called and cancelled any scheduled appointment. The information sheet on the little girl's family indicated that the father was a physician, the mother was attending graduate school at a nearby university, and her older sisters were in college.

Jill's mother had recently called the teacher and said, "I am taking Jill out of school and sending her to live with her grandmother in another state." This was two months before the end of the school year. When Miss Ames asked where the school records should be sent, the mother told her that Jill would not be attending school where she was going. Miss Ames then insisted on a conference with both parents before they withdrew Jill from school.

During the conference, the teacher told the parents that the decision was obviously theirs to make but that she thought it would be in Jill's best interest to keep her in school. She also said, "Jill needs the interaction with the other children. Furthermore, her relationship with me is very important to your child and should not be severed at this time." The father agreed with the teacher that Jill should stay in school, but the mother stated firmly, "I never wanted Jill and I am not going to let the requirements of caring for her keep me from pursuing my graduate degree which is very important to me." She added, "Miss Ames, this may shock you but while I love my child, I did not and do not now want her. Frankly, she is a burden to the whole family." Miss Ames tried to communicate to the parents that they were not making their love for Jill known to her, because the girl often said that her Mommy did not love her. The teacher pointed out that Jill frequently begged to stay at school after closing time, because she was afraid no one would be at home when she got there.

When the parents left, they said they would call Miss Ames over the weekend and tell her their decision. The father did call to say that his wife insisted that Jill go to her grandmother's to live. A week later, the mother brought Jill back to school, saying, "She has been so unhappy that the grandmother insisted she return home." In this situation, as it developed, there was always the danger that Miss Ames would exceed her responsibilities because of a lack of objectivity. Her concern for Jill and the belief that she was not getting a fair deal almost caused her to argue with the parents over a decision that was theirs to make. She had the right to express her opinion and point to possibilities, but nothing more.

A third concern, and a very widespread one, is the fact that a great many teachers come out of a middle or upper-middle class background, while their students come out of every class of society. Such teachers have values that are not recognized or accepted by some students. One area in which there are substantial variations in values and behavior is that of sexual attitudes and sexual behavior. Elkin (1989) emphasizes that people in the upper and middle classes are more apt to accept masturbation, heavy petting, and liberalized sex play among married couples, while disapproving of pre-marital sex relations and prostitution. Conversely, persons in the lower income and educational levels are more likely to accept prostitution, and pre-marital sex, but to reject excessive sex play between spouses, and to consider heavy petting as unnecessary. As with all generalizations, there are cautions and, in this area, it is necessary to recognize differences among nationalities and religions in defining what is acceptable.

It is not a teacher's right or responsibility to impose values on the children with whom they are working, or their parents, regardless of socio-economic backgrounds. For example, throughout history, most families around the world have been male-dominated, or patriarchal. This paternalism was supported by religious doctrines and practices, by the economics of the man as the wage-earner, and by laws that substantiated the dominance of the male. Patriarchy in its many forms in the Judeo-Christian world, has been under attack by civil rights groups, feminists, legislators, and professional organizations, to mention a few. However, children entering nursery school, Head Start, Day Care, Kindergarten, or any other program may come from families that retain aspects of this attitude and corresponding behavior, namely, that the male should have preference. It is also possible that some teachers possess a patriarchal orientation from their own background, in spite of any training to the contrary they may have received. For those who work with young children, an awareness of history is a valuable resource. It provides a basis for interpreting behavior of young people who come from parental teaching of various backgrounds. Such awareness will provide a sensitivity for the teacher that any attempts to modify the behavior of male children who assert a male superiority, or female children who demonstrate a passivity, can cause serious problems for the child at home. There will also be children who make no distinction as to rights, while some children may be confused as to masculine and feminine roles as they pertain to mother and father. Teachers have the contradictory responsibility of understanding where the different children are "coming from" in various situations, helping them to reconcile role definitions in play groups and learning situations, and to work with parents without offending them. A grasp of the origins of particular behavior provides respect, even while rejecting the propriety of such behaviors.

The teacher may find, in individual conferences, that parents are not willing to openly discuss their concerns, or that they want to talk about some concern, but are afraid or embarrassed to do so. It may be possible to relieve parents' anxieties or guilt feelings by giving them factual information about such topics as masturbation and sexual play, if a concern is present and the parents asked for help. For example, the parents might be worried about their child's sex play at home, and also its possible effect upon his or her school behavior. To help the parents with such a sensitive topic, it is essential for the teacher to be a good listener. If one listens carefully and offers encouragement, he or she can determine their real concerns and allow them to discuss it thoughtfully and comfortably. If the teacher is too aggressive, it may stop all communication. If one is encouraging and understanding, he or she will learn more approaches that will be most helpful in working with the child in the classroom.

Parents' concerns sometimes involve problems that have a psychological basis, some of which have a definite relationship to sexual identity. Sexual identity is not usually a major problem for parents of little girls, except in extreme cases, because some amount of "tomboyish" activity is acceptable. It is true that a mother who is a single parent will want her female child to be aware of the male role in the family. But the more serious problem is that of the single female parent who has a male child, because he does not have an adult male to observe. This is also of concern to a divorced parent because an opposite sex model is not available, at least on a regular basis. It also applies to the mother whose husband is deceased, or overseas in the military service, or away from home for extended periods. It is less common, but the single male parent with a female child is also faced with the need to make sure that the little girl has plenty of opportunity to learn female roles. A female teacher or caretaker is a partial solution, but she does not exhibit various behaviors of a female in the home and in the presence of males. In these cases, the teacher is in a position to observe the child's behavior in school and determine whether some assistance is in order. If the teacher believes that the young child is developing sexual identification normally, he or she can help the parent to relax. If the teacher feels that the child is having problems, he or she can work with the parent to help the child. The vignette of Carl in Chapter IV is an example of a teacher's successful effort in this area.

There are also physiological problems that the parents may desire to discuss with the teacher. For example, the young boy whose testicles have not descended into the scrotum, or the little girl who has extra nipples on her body. While these are not common conditions, they do occur, as do others of this nature, and even though the parents have had medical counselling and guidance, they may need the relief from anxiety and guilt they can obtain by discussing the situation with the teacher. The teacher should assure them that the condition, whatever it is, has existed before, and that young children in the pre-school program will be able to take it in stride if it is not over-emphasized. The teacher can also assure them that if problems do develop, they will be consulted and they will work together to solve them.

QUESTIONS FOR DISCUSSION

1. How can the following situations best be handled in pre-school?

    a. When a mature child asks a sophisticated question about sex and reproduction.

    b. When creative play becomes sexual in orientation.

    c. When the teacher is unprepared to answer a question or cope with a situation in the pre-school setting.

2.   How do you interpret Grams when he writes that infants and young children have their basic needs fulfilled by others?

3.   If a child enters kindergarten with a "damaged ego," what are the responsibilities of the teacher to "repair" it?

4.   Discuss any special considerations in the sexual development of exceptional children; (a) with regard to the child, (b) with regard to other children, and (c) with regard to the parents.

5.   What are the most important qualities for a teacher when working with aggressive young children? With neurologically-impaired youngsters? With uninformed and immature young children?

6.   Discribe a problem with the developing sexuality of a young child and structure a conference with the parents for resolving it.

CHAPTER REFERENCES

Grams, A. (1970). Sex education: a guide for teachers. Danville, IL: The Interstate Printers and Publishers.

D'Evelyn, K. (1970). Developing mentally healthy children. Washington, DC: Study Action Publication, American Association of Elementary, Kindergarten, Nursery Educators.

Morgan, E.L. (1989). Talking with parents when concerns come up. Young Children, 44: 52-56.

Elkin, F. (1989). The child and society: the process of socialization. (5th Ed.) New York: Random House.

CHAPTER III

SOME COMPLEXITIES AND PROBLEMS IN THE DEVELOPMENT OF SEXUALITY

The most common areas that perplex parents and teachers in dealing with sexuality of the pre-school child are communicating about masturbation, nudity in the home, sex talk and sex play, and adult sex behaviors which may affect the young child directly, such as child molesting and persons exposing themselves in public. The most valuable parental qualities in dealing with the latter areas are a calmness about the child's experiences and a non-punishing, matter-of-fact attitude. In a general sense, this is true in all the activities and situations that will be discussed in this chapter. It is also helpful for a teacher to know the methods the parents use in handling any of these situations when the child enters school so that reinforcement can be provided for sound parental judgment. The teacher can also help to correct problems and make adjustments when a situation has been handled poorly or the consequences are undesirable.

SEXUAL BEHAVIORS THAT MAY ANNOY, IRRITATE, OR FRIGHTEN PARENTS, TEACHERS, AND OTHER ADULTS

Communications: Right Words, Right Time, Right Place

One of the basic problems for parents and educators of the pre-school child is their inability to communicate with the child about sex or sexual matters. This may be due to a lack of interest in discussing sex, lack of knowledge about the sexual behavior of children, or lack of knowledge of the techniques and language to use when attempting to talk with the young child. The inability to communicate with young children may be due to the failure of adults to be comfortable with their own sexuality.

The pre-school child may receive information about sexuality from the family television set as well as his peers and older children. Even if parents are vaguely conscious of the growing sexual awareness in their child, they may feel inadequate to cope with the situation; consequently, these parents do not acknowledge the existence of the need for communication. Mary Calderone (1966) believes that part of the communication barrier between parents and children is that the parent has not accepted his or her own sexuality. She points out that the infant and young child receive their sex education from the impressions and attitudes received from the adults around them and from the contacts with radio, television, and pictures in newspapers and magazines. She concluded that this distorted and unsatisfactory basis for sexual understanding is hardly offset by the one time effort many parents force themselves to make to tell their children "the facts of life."

Figure 3-1 *(Photo courtesy of Diane Wilson)*

Unquestionably, the parents should be the first and foremost sex educators. They should provide factual information to the child and impart the capacity for love and the ability to integrate sex as a creative force throughout life. In an article, "Sex Education for Parents," Looft (1971) says that parents who grew up under restricted conditions may feel that sex is a highly sensitive topic, difficult to discuss with their children. He also notes that the generation gap is most conspicuous with regard to matters of sex when it comes to teenagers and their parents. Surveys indicate that both groups are more comfortable talking together on any other subject than sex. Most parents want their children to know and understand the facts of sex and to enjoy sex wisely and thoroughly but they have trouble expressing it.

If effective communication about sex and all the other major aspects of life is crucial for a good relationship between parents and their children, it follows that the earlier such communicating begins, the easier it will be for both. From birth onward when the parent talks with the infant and child the correct terms for parts of the body and bodily functions should be used. This will not only make later communication consistent from year to year, but will also give the child a "natural" manner of speaking to incorporate into his developing language patterns. It makes more sense to call a baby boy's sex organ a penis than a "wee-wee." At some age, he will have to stop saying "wee-wee," so it should be easier to start him with the correct terminology. More importantly, using correct words helps eliminate many of the artificial barriers surrounding discussions of sexual matters.

Jamie

In the last few years, a definite trend has developed toward encouraging more accuracy in the language children use when discussing sexual portions of their body and the processes of body elimination. This may be due to a growing awareness among young parents of the value of giving children the correct terms to use. Many children entering kindergarten today are using proper sexual terminology; however, at the beginning of each school year the teacher usually encounters a new word or phrase which she has to decipher. This happened to Mrs. Blue when six-year-old Jamie shouted for her to come to him in the bathroom. When she entered, Jamie was sitting on the toilet. He said, "I went 'grunt grunt'." This wasn't too difficult to interpret for Mrs. Blue who answered, "I understand, your bowels moved, but why did you call me?" Jamie then stood up and told her that she had to help him. Puzzled, Mrs. Blue asked why. He explained, "I can go 'grunt grunt' by myself, but I can't wipe myself." Although

Mrs. Blue had helped many children in various ways with bathroom problems, she had never encountered this situation. Quickly evaluating it, she told Jamie that, since he was now in school, he should learn to wipe himself with the toilet paper. She calmly told him to try, and she would help if necessary, but she thought he could do it. He did, and after he washed his hands, Mrs. Blue hugged him and said that now he could probably manage using the toilet paper himself.

Afterwards, the teacher telephoned the mother, related the incident and asked if she had handled the situation satisfactorily. Jamie's mother said that despite her worry she had been too ashamed of the child's behavior to mention it to the teacher. She explained that several months before, when Jamie had diarrhea, he had soiled his hands and subsequently refused to wipe himself. The mother thought that his constipation might somehow be related to the soiling incident. She praised Mrs. Blue's handling of the incident and said that she would insist that Jamie wipe himself in the future. Several weeks later, she called to say that both Jamie's reluctance to wipe himself and his constipation had disappeared. By this time he was going to the bathroom at school with no problems. In his case, the immature language was less of a problem than his behavior. Jamie's request for help, however, is typical of the freedom with which pre-school children talk about sexual matters and elimination unless they have been taught that this subject is "dirty" and/or "bad."

All adults who talk with the young child about sex should do so in the same manner as they would about anything else which is of interest. The child is entitled to simple, honest answers to each question. It is true that the young child often asks questions at times when it is embarrassing or inconvenient to answer. A child will accept the explanation that an answer will be given later if the parent's policy is to do what has been promised. Even when a parent answers the child's question, the same question may be asked many more times. Often the child is seeking more information than was received the last time, but sometimes the answer has been forgotten.

If the subject of pregnancy, reproduction, or menstruation comes up normally in the family discussions or family situations, there is no reason for young children to be excluded or their questions to be left unanswered. For example, a little girl will accept the fact of menstruation as a very normal function both now and when she reaches puberty if the subject has not been taboo during her formative early years. This does not mean that the child should be subject to discussions among adults concerning all the biological and possibly negative aspects of menstruation. Rather, if a little girl sees a sanitary napkin and questions its use, she should be given a simple, direct answer.

Some parents act if as if they can eliminate sex as an aspect of the child's life by explaining nothing. They assume that absence of any discussion is desirable, but that is not correct. When parents do not give their children verbal instruction, they really communicate to them that sex is a topic so mysterious, so unimportant, or so difficult to discuss that the child will not learn about it from them. While this may be more likely to happen to the older child, it also applies to the young child as well. It should be recognized that parental behavior in the home is a means of communicating whether sex is discussed or not. The child learns through observation that there are differences between the sexes with regard to both anatomy and roles played. It will be observed whether parents are affectionate with each other, the forms that any affection takes, whether they accept their roles and accompanying responsibility with enthusiasm or reluctance, and many other domestic situations and activities. Such observations constitute a significant part of sex education or education for sexuality of the young child.

Young children do engage in sex-related activities, some of which often cause concern on the part of parents. As stated above, some problems are too complex for parents and teachers to cope with so they should turn to professionals for help. For example, a child who has been sexually molested by an adult may exhibit such trauma that guidance from a professional psychologist, psychiatrist, or other qualified person is needed promptly. Most problems of a sexual nature with regard to the young child, however, are problems largely in the eyes of the parents, since the child may be involved in behavior that is part of the normal sequence in the process of developing a sexuality. Consequently, parents and teachers need to become much more knowledgeable in this area in order to discriminate normal behavior from that which is deviant or unusual.

Masturbation

Masturbation is a common behavior and usually occurs through the young child's interest in touching the genitals which causes a degree of pleasure and so he or she continues to engage in such behavior. Masturbation does not result in blindness, cause pimples, or contribute to poor sexual adjustment in adult life, nor does it result in insanity; all things that many adults were once taught to believe. A child can develop unhealthy feelings of anxiety and guilt, however, if punished or constantly scolded or threatened for masturbating. The situation is complicated by the fact that masturbation is considered unacceptable public behavior in our society, even for a young child.

The medical profession is in general agreement that while masturbation produces no harmful physical effects, it can cause psychological damage if the child is made to feel that something wrong has occurred and, therefore, has been bad. Many experts are currently taking the position that masturbation may be regarded as a normal part of sexual maturing and is common rather than unusual behavior. This is not to imply that this is only true for young children but can be applied to the population at large. The following comment in Sexuality and Man (1970, p. 63), is appropriate here, "Although masturbation is usually considered to be a phenomenon of adolescence, many boys and girls discover orgasm long before puberty. Prior to puberty, and not uncommonly in the pre-school child, the male, like the female, is capable of orgasm even though it is not accompanied by ejaculation."

The word "masturbation" makes many people anxious and uncomfortable, and they will avoid the word altogether. The term itself, as generally used, refers to sexual self-stimulation that leads to orgasm. Two other terms, both somewhat obsolete, that are applied to such behavior are "autoeroticism" and "self-abuse." The application here will be restricted to mean the handling or touching of their genitals that young children engage in but is not directed specifically toward the achievement of orgasm as such because that has no meaning to them.

For young children generally, masturbation is sporadic if it is engaged in at all. It is therefore a problem primarily if the parents create one by being unduly concerned, thereby creating guilt feelings and anxiety in the child. If a young child is discovered to be masturbating excessively it is likely to be an indication that there are other conditions which are bothering the child. Excessive masturbation is when the child engages in it much of the time when he is not otherwise occupied. These children are usually able to be identified easily in contrast with the child who only masturbates occasionally. The conditions that are often associated with excessive masturbation include emotional problems, mental retardation, and neurological handicaps. It is important to identify the child's basic problem first. For example, there are children who should be on drug therapy once the problem is diagnosed as neurological impairment. Prescribed medication sould help control the tensions and frustrations such a child experiences, and reduce or eliminate the need for masturbation as a tension reliever. For a child without such a complex problem, the child's physician should check the possibility of skin irritation on the genitals.

While students of human sexuality concur with medical doctors that masturbation is not physically harmful, they do differ about how parents should cope with such behavior. Arnstein (1967) points out that we are often distressed by this behavior of our child because as parents we can't toss aside our own emotions or upbringing. She also believes that even if we could do so, we would still have to come to terms with the fact that society disapproves or thinks the practice should be engaged in privately. Arnstein adds that it is probably best to ignore occasional masturbation. If a child is happy and secure, an interest in one's own body becomes only a minor part of the total life. However, excessive masturbation is usually a sign that the child is troubled emotionally and needs help.

Calderone and Johnson (1981) believe that the infant is born with a sexual response and shortly after birth, the male will begin to experience erections and the female will show signs of fluid in the vaginal area. It is common and normal for the young child to touch the genital areas; the value is vital for finding a pleasurable sensation in one's own body, so there is no reason to interfere. It is now accepted that touching the genitals by infants and young children is an integral part of the body's responsive system. Such behavior is not taught, but will come naturally on the part of the child and can generally be ignored by the parents. Spock (1988) says exploration of the genitals at one year of age is normal as an aspect of curiosity and growing sense of self. He adds that experimentation and sex play are very common with children three to six years of age. Certainly scolding or punishment is not called for in any way. In children approaching school age, perhaps the primary need is to establish the private nature of masturbation and to discourage excessive activity at the expense of growing up. Parents can quite properly say to their children, "I know it feels good to touch yourself on the vagina (or penis), but it should only be done when you are alone and not by anyone else."

Levine (1968), believes that most children, even if they have not been directly scolded or threatened, seem to sense quite early that masturbation is not acceptable public behavior. They see that it is not done openly or publicly by older children and adults. It is recommended that if the child is bothered by masturbation, help him or her in any way you can to find other satisfactions. The child may be too inactive, or have rest periods that are too long. The child may need to be occupied in new ways, or to have more time and affection from his or her parents. If masturbation continues to interfere with the widening of his or her interests and activities, getting professional help might be wise. In any event, avoid harsh criticism or frightening threats and don't try to "talk it out" even sympathetically. Usually a child doesn't want to talk about masturbation and shouldn't be forced to. If the child feels that you enjoy him or her and like to do things with him or her, he or she will sense your support and understanding.

In the opinion of Calderone and Johnson (1981), masturbation is a prelude to and a preparation for sex in a mature way, and its most important function is its role in developing a strong sense of self. It is estimated that over 95 percent of all males and about 75 percent of all females have masturbated at some period during their lifetime. It is known that some people masturbate only before they have the opportunity for sexual satisfaction with a partner. Others practice masturbation with some degree of frequency throughout their lifetime, both with and without a partner. The practice is also utilized during periods of a partner's absence, or after the loss of a partner because of illness, death, or various other causes.

Some authorities take the position that masturbation may be beneficial for later sexual adjustment in marriage, since masturbation trains and develops the senses and organs which will later function during sexual intercourse. Furthermore, if parents make their children feel guilty, they may inhibit their children's feelings and cause further use of their sexual organs to become ridden with anxiety. For such children, the result may be a failure to transform adolescent sexual feelings into mature love.

Parents and teachers are jointly responsible for helping the young child learn and be aware of the distinction that every individual must learn to make between what is acceptable as public and private behavior. While this can be accomplished by explaining to the child what unacceptable public behavior is, thus avoiding any sense of anxiety and guilt in the child, it is often unnecessary since young children are quite perceptive and often sense their parent's concern by their behavior. Many children of kindergarten age have already recognized that this is unacceptable behavior in public as indicated by the fact that they masturbate unobtrusively rather than openly.

Nancy

Taking action on such apparently simple although annoying behavior can sometimes reveal much deeper problems which can be alleviated if treated promptly. Nancy was a neurologically-impaired child who had not yet learned that masturbation in public is unacceptable behavior. During Nancy's child-parent-teacher conference, the teacher observed that she was hyperactive, highly distractible, very large for her age, and had poor gross motor coordination, but had an excellent vocabulary, talking easily and intelligently. While Nancy was playing alone in the play house the mother assured the teacher, Miss Eaton, that the child had been spoiled by her older brothers and sisters, but had no problems.

After Kindergarten had been in session three weeks, the mother called Miss Eaton complaining that other children were calling Nancy names. She said that, although Nancy did not seem upset, she did not like her child called "Nancy pants." Miss Eaton answered that she was aware of the name-calling and suggested a conference for that afternoon.

What Miss Eaton did not tell the mother on the phone was that she was less concerned with the name calling than with Nancy's constant masturbation during quiet activities. The other children had noticed and were openly watching. A few had commented about her mannerism of flipping her dress up.

As a first step in resolving the problem of the masturbation, Miss Eaton called the school physician and, without revealing the child's name, asked if she should discuss Nancy's behavior with the mother and perhaps suggest that the child wear tight pants to school. The physician encouraged her to be frank with the mother and suggest the change of clothing. He stated that although Nancy would probably substitute another behavior for the masturbation, it was not in the best interests of the other children for her to continue masturbating so openly.

Miss Eaton explained her other concerns about the child and asked if she might have some neurological impairment. When he learned what the teacher had observed and why she was concerned, he advised her to tell the mother about their phone conversation and her concerns and suggest an appointment. The doctor explained that if necessary he would refer the child to a pediatric neurologist in the area.

When the mother arrived for the conference, she agreed with Miss Eaton's preliminary remark that honesty and frankness were the only way they could help Nancy. After they had discussed how Miss Eaton would handle the name-calling, the teacher asked the mother whether she was aware that Nancy masturbated. The mother did know and she was greatly concerned because Nancy seemed unaware that her behavior was unacceptable. She said that she had lain awake worrying about the problems that Nancy's behavior would create for her in school.

Miss Eaton told the mother about talking to the school doctor with anonymity and that he agreed with the solution of having Nancy start the next day to wear tights and continue for the rest of the year. The mother agreed and the first day she dug a hole in them, but stopped masturbating at school from that day on. To resolve the name calling, Miss Eaton said she would have group discussion on the subject and stop any child who began calling another names. During the conference Miss Eaton explained that her observations suggested that Nancy might have a learning disorder problem. The teacher then recommended a visit to a pediatrician giving him all the information about Nancy she could.

At that, the mother began to cry, explaining that she had worried since Nancy's birth about the child's development, since she knew that her problem-laden pregnancy plus a long and difficult delivery could cause brain damage. The mother's experience as a nursery school teacher and with the older siblings convinced her that her daughter has some problems. She had taken the child to several physicians and to the child study clinic at a local university, but in every case Nancy's development was considered within the normal range, with above average intellectual development. The mother promised to call her child's pediatrician immediately. She requested any help available from the school, and thanked Miss Eaton for her recommendations as she had long blamed herself for having a baby when she was too old to rear a child properly.

Miss Eaton assured the mother that Nancy reflected an excellent home environment with plenty of love, security and intellectual stimulation. She added that identification of a possible neurological or learning disorder problem should be done during the kindergarten year so that the child could be placed in the best learning environment the next year, with special help if necessary.

Both mother and teacher initiated several more conferences on Nancy's progress during the year. The pediatric neurologist to whom Nancy's pediatrician referred her reported to the school that Nancy did have neurological impairment. Another study by the school psychologist indicated that in first grade Nancy would need special help, which she received. In second grade she entered a learning-disorder class for part of her school day.

The initial problem of name-calling which brought the mother to school led to early identification of the learning disorder, led to help from specialists, and good cooperation and communication between the home and school. Consequently, Nancy is doing well academically and will soon enter middle school. Despite her academic success, Nancy is emotionally and socially retarded, and exhibits strange behaviors that make her peers uncomfortable. As a result, she has difficulty in relating to them. This inability to relate indicates the absence of a healthy sexuality. Although she may not have the opportunity for normal dating in adolescence, it is possible that she will mature in time and be able to give and find happiness.

Essa (1990) believes it is important for both parents and the school staff to give careful thought as to why a child is engaged in self-stimulation. She points out that the behavior could be due to arousal from an abusive situation. Another explanation could be that the child is reacting to anxiety and masturbating is a source of relief. Perhaps the child has a bladder or genital infection and the behavior is an easing of pain or itching. The most likely explanation, however, is that the child enjoys the sensation. It would be wise to talk with the child in a non-threatening manner and listen carefully to the answers. If a teacher observes repeated masturbation, it is important to contact the parents and share observations with each other.

One specific thing the parents can do is try to observe their child when he or she masturbates and try to analyze what kinds of situations evoke this behavior. If the child is bored, lonely, or possibly feels rejected, the basic action is to meet the child's immediate needs. If a child chooses certain times or situations such as at nap time or watching television, the parent can suggest substitutions, e.g., replace television with a story-telling session. At bed time, the parent could tell bed time stories or alter the situation in any manner that would induce sleep. In any case, the parents should realize that masturbation is common behavior in the pre-school child and generally has no long-range significance.

Sex Talk and Sex Play

An area of real concern for many parents is their child's indulgence in "sex talk" or "sex play." It is interesting that adults may consider themselves quite fair and open-minded and yet they quickly become uncomfortable if they hear a small child utter four letter words, including those they use themselves. Inevitably, a youngster will hear some of the vulgar, coarse, obscene, or unacceptable language from their parents, their peers, or other persons. They may or may not know or feel that the word is unacceptable in some way but will nevertheless repeat it over and over. Sometimes this is done to get a reaction from the parents. Young children explore in a variety of ways and it is common to use trial and error - to test words to see what happens - with both adults and children. Furthermore, any child who is seeking attention will often use negative methods to achieve it from the parents and sex talk is usually an effective way.

Sex talk can be handled by parents in the same way as other sexual matters. Give the child a direct, honest answer that the word is not acceptable, explain what it means in a calm, unemotional manner, and that a continued use will cause problems at school, in public and at home. This approach is only necessary if the child repeatedly uses the words, as sex talk is usually sporadic, and has no meaning to the child unless the parents display shock or anger. Sex talk is much more common today than in the past because the child is exposed to it through television, videos, and movies. It is also true that the child is more verbal and knowledgeable about sex in general than in the past. Nevertheless, small children will tattle on their peers who use sex talk on the playground or around the neighborhood, whether the words used are of the four letter kind or the proper terms.

Larry

A group of four and five year old children were playing on the playground after school. Larry's mother was nearby but was not involved in the play. Suddenly Larry said, "If we're going to play kick ball I'm going to take off my shirt. I'm hot." He proceeded to remove his shirt and several other boys followed suit. One boy commented that he had nipples and little boobs and so did Larry. Larry replied that everyone has them, and turned to a little girl standing nearby and said, "Julia, take off your blouse and show us your boobs." Julia retorted angrily, "I will not. I'm not supposed to show any part of me that is not covered by my bathing suit." Jack volunteered that his mother had real big boobs and that it felt good to put his head between them. Larry then said, "When I push real hard, I can make my navel stick out." He demonstrated and all the other boys began to try to make their navels stick out. At this point, Larry's mother interrupted and explained that it was dangerous to do that because it might cause a hernia and also explained what a hernia was in elementary terms. The children listened and then returned to their game of kickball.

In a sense, play is a child's occupation, a necessary part of learning about life. It enables a child to establish a sexual identity, learn appropriate sex roles and to expand upon limited experiences by imitating the behaviors of the family and others with whom he or she has contact. During their play, children learn acceptable and unacceptable ways of doing and saying things from their peers, parents, and others. The teacher's responsibility is not to dominate the play of children but to offer guidance, provide good equipment and accessories, and to provide a variety of learning experience that children can incorporate into their play. (See Figure 3-2)

Figure 3-2 *(Photo courtesy of Diane Wilson)*

Young children build a lot of their play upon experiences at home and at pre-school. Parents and teachers are continually providing learning experiences, some routine and some special events, such as a family's vacation in the mountains or at the seaside. Television is also a source of activities for play but while some programs are excellent, others have some negative, even dangerous aspects. When the "Three Stooges" movies were popular, a teacher never knew when small fingers would jab someone in the eye.

Billy

The fact that young children are sexual beings and their sexuality is continuing to develop makes it inevitable that some of their play will be sexual in nature. Both parents and teachers need to be generally aware of the direction of young children's play so they can stop or re-direct activities which are not constructive in any way. Mrs. Beck faced such a situation when Billy and a group of his friends were in the playhouse. Billy had made a penis out of modeling clay and said, "Let's play the way I saw people acting in a movie last night. Daddy was mad at me for sneaking downstairs and watching the picture in which people were doing strange things and running around with no clothes on." Mrs. Beck quickly announced clean-up time and went to the playhouse to help the children.

Later, on the playground, Billy talked about the picture with his teacher and said, "It really was weird because all these naked people were touching and kissing each other all over their bodies." Mrs. Beck listened, told him matter-of-factly that when he was sent to bed, he should stay there, and went on. The student teacher who overheard the conversation asked Mrs. Beck whether she planned to talk with the parents. The teacher replied that, while she had the responsibility of stopping play in the classroom if it seemed undesirable, she did not have the right to become involved with a home situation unless it caused a problem at school. She added that the parents were probably concerned with the fact that Billy had seen part of the stag movie and had handled it as they thought best. The student teacher then asked why she did not talk more to the little boy to alleviate any possible trauma. Mrs. Beck said that while he obviously had a need to tell someone about his experience, he did not display either anger or guilt. She also pointed out that she could not explain to Billy what he had seen or why his parents were watching the film. This is primarily a family situation and should be handled at home so the teacher changed the direction of the children's play and pursued the matter no farther.

Sally

Play situations involving modeling clay and sex symbols are not very common but "having a baby" occurs quite frequently when young children get together. Sally talked freely for a number of weeks about her mother's pregnancy. On the day after the delivery, Sally carried a doll under her dress and told the other children in the play house that her baby would be born that day. Juan was assigned to be the doctor but no one seemed to know what the doctor was supposed to do. Sally said,"I know the doctor helps the baby come out of the vagina but I will just drop the baby on the floor when it is born." Then she said, "Juan, you can help weigh her. I know the doctor always does that in his office." As she was leaving the "doctor's office," she dropped the doll on the floor. All the children in the playhouse gathered around and exclaimed over the beautiful baby. They called the teacher over who also praised the baby but gave no indication that she was aware of their play and the way it was carried out.

Another common activity in children's play is the investigation and exploratory research into comparative anatomy. For the child of three, this is result of natural curiosity and it will be done quite openly. Often children of five or six, however, have learned that adults are likely to disapprove of such play; therefore they are likely to conceal it from older persons. Actually children of five and six are often quite uncomfortable while examining and touching each other's bodies, and at times even go out of their way to get caught. When parents or teachers discover children in such touch and feel behaviors, it should be accepted as play with no hidden or suspicious motive and ended by suggesting some other activity. There is no reason for scolding, shaming, or punishing a child. This makes the child feel guilty without knowing exactly what has been done that was wrong. It may make for anxious feelings, or it may make the whole area one of much greater excitement than it ever was before. This also presents an excellent opportunity to explain to the young child that certain parts of one's body are private and should only be touched by others for good reason.

It is suggested by Money and Tucker (1975) that when parents intervene in young children's sex play, they should not attempt to stop it. The children will likely continue it at a more convenient time and if it is presented as evil, the child may get an interpretation of a sex related activity that will become a detriment in the normal development of his or her sexuality. There are cultures that have been studied by anthropologists in which young children are encouraged to explore their genitals and to pretend to enter into sexual intercourse as a preparation for adulthood. It is claimed that the people who follow this way of life are free of impotency and other psychological disorders that are common in Western culture. This behavior is not accepted in the American view of child-rearing but Money and Tucker (1975) believe we should seek a way to manage the sexuality of children more effectively but certainly not try to squelch it entirely. One approach would be to ignore the experimentation of young children entirely and cease to interpret their actions as having the same meaning they would if indulged in by adults or even older children. It is recommended that any approach should eliminate those definitions which create guilt feelings, anxieties and neurotic fears.

Jay

> Jay's mother was working in the yard when her neighbor came running over. She was quite upset, and said,"I just found Jay on top of Delores in the garden behind the garage and they were pretending to have sexual intercourse, and were hugging and kissing. What in the world are we going to do?" In this case, the little boy was six years old and the little girl was four. The two agitated mothers were good friends and discussed the situation reasonably calmly. They agreed it was not a crime but was part of the children's attempt to grow up, but were most uncertain as to where the children got their ideas. After a long discussion, they decided they would not tell their husbands, they would not scold the children, and they would supervise the children more closely and prevent a recurrence. The two mothers also agreed that if there was a reoccurrence, they would have to discuss the behavior and its unacceptability with the children.

There are several questions that can be raised by this vignette. First, why did the mothers decide not to tell their husbands about the incident? Why did they delay in discussing the situation with the children unless there is a second time? What might have happened if the two neighbors had not been good friends? Suppose they had had numerous disagreements over the years, would they have been so calm and rational in reacting? Perhaps more to the point, what should a teacher do if this behavior is discovered in the closet of the schoolroom or in a corner of the playground? From the standpoint of the young people, this was probably a pleasurable event. Where did they learn it? Could imitative sex behavior be an imitation of something they had seen on television, or in their own home, or in the neighborhood? Teachers who are involved with young people should be prepared for behaviors that they believe should not occur. Young children are receptive to new things, they are imitative, they are curious, but they rarely, if ever, have ulterior motives. Teachers must not be shocked, but must cope with such situations calmly, even though it is on the spur of the moment. It is on occasions like this that a teacher should be appreciative if she is familiar with the sexual development of the young child.

The area of sex talk and sex play is one in which the parents are often prone to project their own anxieties and fears into their children's behavior. Because of emotional reactions, they may cause the child to feel bad for engaging in the situation. For the young person, this type of behavior is sporadic, a part of their exploration of human behavior, and a curiosity that is usually not harmful. There is a need for guidance and supervision on a continuous basis because young children do not have the experience to differentiate good from bad nor do they appreciate the need to conform to society's standards. Sex play is not in itself destructive, but it can become so if one child is exploited by another. This is especially true when a younger child is exploited by an older one. In its essence, sex talk and sex play are only harmful when carried to extremes, or persist repeatedly over time, or take unusual or aberrant forms.

ADULT BEHAVIORS THAT AFFECT CHILDREN, MORE OR LESS

Nudity In The Home

Parents with young children will inevitably have to face the question of letting their child see them nude, especially the parent of the opposite sex. Some people like to walk around their own home in the nude, or wander around the bedroom after a shower, or even take their child into the shower with them. These are family decisions and create problems if the parents disagree about when or where, or if awareness of the behavior begins to extend beyond the home.

Regardless of the family position, it is almost impossible for the young child not to see one or both parents undressed at some time or other. For the parents to avoid this would require extreme measures of which the child would certainly become aware sooner or later. If doors are locked or the child is screamed at, the situation is certain to be thought of as strange, although the reason will not be clear. If the parents show embarrassment when caught off guard, it will reinforce the child's belief that something is wrong with nudity. This could extend to the child's self-evaluation, although this would be somewhat unusual.

Mary

During her orientation conference Mrs. Lee expressed concern that there was no lock on the bathroom door. She asked how privacy was insured for five year olds like her daughter, Mary, in the nursery. The teacher explained, "I do have rules for the use of the bathroom. The children are instructed to use the bathroom singly, to close the door, and when they finish, to wash their hands and leave the door open when they come out. However, I do not think it advisable for a small child to lock the door from the inside."

Mrs. Lee replied, "I hope the rules are always enforced, because I feel strongly that using the bathroom is a private matter. In our home, this is a rule followed firmly by all family members from the age of three. My whole family also dresses privately because I believe it is a sin to view other people in the nude." She closed by saying, "I want my children to be as modest as my husband and I. We have never seen each other in a state of nudity." The teacher's only comment was to assure Mrs. Lee that she would make an extra effort to insure Mary's privacy.

Several days later the teacher sensed from observing Mary that she needed to use the bathroom to urinate. She quietly asked the girl if she wanted to go, but Mary replied that she could wait, adding, "Mother told me not to use the school bathroom because someone might see me." Mary refused to use the bathroom even when the teacher promised to guard the door. Mary continued to abstain from using the school toilet. One day while she was absorbed in her play, she did urinate and then became hysterical. As soon as the teacher determined the nature of the problem, she calmed Mary down and assured her that many children had such accidents at school. The teacher found her some dry clothes. The bathroom was the only place in which to change, and Mary went into it without protest. When Mrs. Lee came to get her daughter, the teacher told her what had happened and why. She added, "This will probably happen again if you do not give Mary permission to use the school bathroom." Mrs. Lee reluctantly agreed and there were no more such incidents.

Later in the year, Mary's mother was in the classroom when a little boy told the teacher he wanted her to see the boil on his testicles and promptly dropped his pants to the floor. When he went back to his play group, the teacher observed to Mrs. Lee that there are many different styles of family living, as the young boy's family obviously did not share her concern about nudity.

The position of Mary's family on nudity is not a serious one for a small child, as the family is in full agreement on the policy in the home.

In later years, when the little girl begins to take physical education or goes to summer camp or even goes to a public swimming pool, the problems of adjustment may be quite difficult for her. Not only can Mary be exposed to the nudity of others, but even if she can avoid exposing her own body, she may be the object of a considerable amount of ridicule and teasing. In addition, this extreme position is difficult to maintain in marriage, and ultimately, in rearing her own children.

On the other hand, some parents make a point of going nude in front of their children. Doors are not locked and the bathroom is as open as the kitchen. These parents believe that if they are comfortable and relaxed in their nudity, the child will develop a wholesome and matter-of-fact attitude about the human body. They also feel that seeing them nude will satisfy the child's curiosity about the differences between males and females. As the children grow older, the practice of nudity may continue as before or it may begin to modify as the children's friends drop in. (See Figure 3-3)

In families where nudity is not the general practice, parents may still be concerned that their children be aware of the anatomical differences between the sexes. This is more pronounced in families with only one child or with several children of the same sex. There are instances where parents have made arrangements with other parents to create situations whereby their two groups of children of both sexes will have an opportunity to observe the characteristics of boys and girls.

Experts do not agree on whether nudity in the home is an important problem or asset in developing the child's sexuality. Some believe that it may well create complications for the child inasmuch as seeing the nude bodies of the parents may arouse a child's interest in touching, exploring and fondling. It is claimed that these are feelings and desires that, once started, cannot be turned off easily and can be disturbing in many ways. Some children may develop their own modesty standard and parents should respect it unless it is abnormal or interferes with the family routine. The child deserves an explanation if the pattern chosen is unacceptable.

One psychiatrist, A. S. Berger (1970), contends that it is much too stimulating for a little boy to see his mother nude, as such nudity may cause the child to be aroused and stimulated toward a goal of unacceptable fulfillment. He also advises parents to establish the same degree of modesty with their young child, regardless of sex, that they would maintain if their neighbor's seventeen year old daughter were sleeping in their home for a few days. Other psychologists and psychiatrists agree that when parents stroll through the house with no clothes on, it is quite seductive to a child trying to combat Oedipal feelings. It is also stressed that the family that practices nudity in the

When asked by her grandmother why the woman wasn't wearing clothes, the six year old girl responded by saying, "This is you ready to take a shower. You look like this in the front and back."

Figure 3-3 Woman

home must take special efforts to make the child aware of the standards and definitions of society as a whole.

Calderone and Johnson (1981) believe that nudity in the home helps young children appreciate the differences between males and females, especially at the adult level. This knowledge would help the child be more secure of his own sexual identity. However, it is true that some children are uncomfortable with nudity and do not wish to be seen undressing or undressed and this desire should be respected. In recent years, there has undoubtedly been a decline in the opposition to nudity in the home, or elsewhere for that matter. The wide variety of bathing suits and casual clothes, plus an increase in beaches that permit nudity, has reduced the sensitivity to nudity and made people less rejecting of the human body.

It is important that a family be in agreement on the issue of nudity. The parents must be honest about their feelings or the child will detect the falsity in their behavior and the fact that they are uncomfortable. The attitudes toward nudity are likely to be consistent with the attitudes toward sex behavior, and the sexuality of themselves and their children. Some privacy for the adults seems reasonable but a family will have to do whatever is natural and comfortable to them. Money & Tucker (1975, p. 131) write, "Ideally, parents will unostentatiously allow their children to become acquainted, from infancy on, with the nude appearance of family members, juvenile and adult, in the normal course of dressing, undressing, and bathing. Ideally, also they will acquaint their children from an early age, step by step, with information about where babies come from, and how; they will not be evasive about the function of the penis and vagina in intercourse."

About Indecent Exposure

The prevalence of men exposing their sex organs to others, usually females, is not easily determined. As in the case of obscene phone calls, many incidents of indecent exposure are not reported, but how many is not known. This uncertainty applies to exposures to children as well as adults. While such behavior does not involve a physical attack or any kind of follow-up, it is most confusing to a small child who has no idea of what's happening. While no parent wants their child to experience this kind of behavior, normally there will be no negative consequences for the future unless the parents overreact. A great show of emotion or anger may create a sense of fear and anxiety that are not appropriate for the situation. Often the child will treat it as a joke or as an event that is unusual but not as anything important.

Lorna

> Six year old Lorna and her little sister, Sharon, came home from the playground one day and told their mother, "We saw a man across the street while we were coming home and he was really weird. He didn't have any clothes on and he was holding his penis in his hand." The mother did not actually know the people who lived in the house the children mentioned but she did know that a divorced son of the couple had recently come to live with them. She told her two daughters, "He will not hurt you but you must not look across the street in that area until you are past the house, then come on home as usual." The children agreed and there were no further incidents. The little girls mentioned the event once or twice more and then it was forgotten. The mother discussed the exposure case with her husband and they decided not to call the police unless it happened again.

It is desirable for parents to protect their children from such occurrences. It is also desirable, if it happens, to protect the child from unpleasant psychological consequences such as hysteria, nightmares and the like. If the matter is handled calmly and easily, even in a light hearted vein, the child is protected in a sound way. Discuss the experience, explain that the man is sick or something on that order, and tell them to forget it. If a child encounters an exposer, or "flasher" on the way to school and tells the teacher, the teacher should also downplay the incident and inform the parents. However, if there are reports from other parents, or the children report it happening again, then a notification of the police may be in order. In any case, the small child should not think it important or bad, otherwise it may distort some views necessary for his or her sexuality to develop normally.

Sexual Activity By Parents and Others

Sexual foreplay and intercourse by the parents are generally accepted as private behaviors. Regardless of the degree of nudity permitted or encouraged by the various family members, there remains the expectation of privacy during sexual intimacies. Even parents who provide their children with very frank and open educations on sexuality are likely to become disturbed if a child opens the door unexpectedly during sexual activities. An exception exists in the millions of one and two room homes where there are adults and children living together. Privacy is not possible unless all others but the participants are sent outside. In these homes, the sex life of the adults continues but the children are usually ignored, so the nature of the behavior is unexplained.

It seems certain that the exposure of young children to strong sexual themes and activities as developed in much of today's TV programs and movies, along with current Top Ten music and videos, has reduced the confusion and uncertainty that existed previously in children's minds about the world of sex. This has no real bearing on the prevailing standards about privacy in the majority of homes. Neither has it led to any involvement of children in the sex lives of their parents as the widespread rejection of child pornography indicates. Perhaps a major change would be a reduction in any sense of embarrassment or shame by parents if discovered in the sex act by children and probably more understanding by the children. If the child has been taught the "facts of life" in a realistic way, the outcome of the discovery might be utilized as a part of that education.

Young children who have received little or no information about sex activities and do not grasp the significance of what they have seen or been told, are quite likely to be disturbed by what they may observe. The child might think the parents are in a fight and are hurting each other. The child might view the sexual behavior as a game and want to join in. In any case, the situation calls for an explanation, not anger, embarrassment, or confusion. To clarify the sex act as a part of being married, to explain that it is fun and the parents enjoy it, may well suffice until the child is ready for a more sophisticated explanation. Perhaps the primary requirement is that the child be made to appreciate that it is a part of the parent's love for each other above and beyond their love for the children.

The interpretations of two, three, and four year old children who have had limited sex instruction is almost beyond belief. One little boy said his parents were doing "pushups." Some parents tell their children that it is a "Mommy-Daddy" game that they play when the children are not around. Whatever the interpretations by the children and the explanation by the parents, it is important that the sex relationship be defined as normal, as pleasant, and as an integral part of marriage. This should lead to a better sexuality for the child by preparing them for what is to come in the future. If presented intelligently and calmly, sex can easily be accepted by very young children as a part of adult life which they will experience in later years along with so many other things. It is also necessary to explain that this is a family matter and not to be discussed in the neighborhood, as is true of discussions about money, political views, and religious positions. For the neighborhood children to become aware is to provide a topic of gossip in some areas, and a source of irritation where parents do not wish for their children to have this information at this time.

Calderone and Johnson (1981) emphasize that there is no good reason to conceal the fact that parents enjoy each other's sexuality. This does not mean that parents should flaunt their sex lives or debate it as they would the evening news, but rather that they should help the children develop an awareness of sexual involvement as an integral part of marriage but a private part. There is no reason the child should be adversely affected if the parents are discovered engaging in sexual relations unless they show guilt or anger. It may be more difficult for the parents to explain if they are discovered while engaging in oral or anal sex or sadomasochistic activities, but it does not justify a defensive reaction.

All in all, parents and teachers of young children have ample opportunity to guide them and help them grow into mature sexual beings. While this is not an easy task, the rewards are great, culminating when the child attains maturity, marries, has children, and successfully begins the whole cycle again. It would be a serious mistake to conclude that young children are not sexual beings and cannot cope with sex and sexuality. For parents, the approach is very simply to share, tell, and show their child the real meaning of sexuality. For the teacher, the responsibilities are two-fold: to help the parents with their tasks with correct information and proper attitudes, and to work with the child to reinforce a strong and positive growth as a sexual human being in the contemporary world. As noted above, a teacher must avoid giving advice or making judgments that are out of one's areas of expertise - make full use of psychologists, psychiatrists, doctors, and other professionals in working with children and parents.

QUESTIONS FOR DISCUSSION

1. Give some examples of how body language can affect a relationship with a young child both positively and/or negatively.

2. If a teacher is uncomfortable with nudity, masturbation, vulgar or obscene language, and various forms of sexual play, how can he or she learn to build an effective relationship with young children and help them develop a strong sexuality?

3. Are there limits to sex talk and sex play in pre-school settings? If not, why not? If so, what are they and how can they best be communicated to the children?

4. The statement is made that "play is a child's occupation." How

should this be interpreted? What kinds of guidance are called for? What kinds of play might not fit this approach?

5. If a child's behavior with regard to nudity, masturbation, unacceptable language, and other aspects of sexuality are disruptive to the group, e.g., Damon, how does the teacher approach the parents and achieve a resolution of the situation?

6. What are the teacher's responsibilities in the sexual development of a young child? What are a teacher's limitations in this area?

CHAPTER REFERENCES

Arnstein, H. (1967). Your growing child and sex: a parent's guide to the sexual development, education, attitudes, and behavior of the child . . from infancy through adolescence. Indianapolis: Bobbs Merrill.

Berger, S. (1970). Sex education of the young child. Young Children, 25: 266-267.

Calderone, M. (1966). The development of healthy sexuality. The Journal of Health, Physical Education, and Recreation, 37: 28-32.

Calderone, M. & E. Johnson (1981). The family book about sexuality. New York: Harper and Row.

Essa, E. (1990). A practical guide to solving preschool behavior problems (2nd ed.). Albany, NY: Delmar Publishers Inc.

Levine, M. (1968). What to tell your child about sex. New York: E.P. Dutton.

Looft, W.R. (1971). Sex education for parents. The Journal for School Health, 41: 433-437.

Money, J. & P. Tucker (1975). Sexual signatures: on being a man or a woman. Boston: Little, Brown and Company.

SIECUS (1970). Sexuality and man. New York: Charles Scribner Sons.

Spock, B. (1988). Dr. Spock on parenting: sensible advice from America's most trusted child care expert. New York: Simon and Schuster.

CHAPTER IV

WHO AM I?

MASCULINE AND FEMININE

It was pointed out earlier that maleness is determined genetically. Now the next question, is this also true of masculinity? Is a male always masculine? Are all males masculine in the same way and to the same degree? Similar questions can be raised with regard to females and femininity. One way to arrive at an answer to such questions is to think of all the qualities that you consider as definitely masculine. This might include big muscles, a deep voice, a heavy beard, an interest in sports, and an interest in math and science. Therefore a male who possessed all these traits in considerable amounts could be defined as a very masculine male while a person who possesses them in very limited quantities would not be very masculine. Of course we know that males do vary in the degree to which these traits are present and also in the quantity to which they have them. This idea is expressed in the figure below whereby one end of the line represents the greatest amount of all the traits you think of as masculine and the other end the least amount of such traits. Every male can be placed somewhere along this line for any individual trait, for any combination of them, or for the total he possesses.

Scale of Masculinity

MOST ---LEAST

It is unlikely that any person would be at either end but that all males would fall between, in other words, more or less masculine rather than completely masculine or not masculine at all. A so-called "sissy" is a boy who has one or more traits that are located toward the Least end of the line, according to someone's list of traits.

Figure 4-1 *(Photo courtesy of Virginia Lively)*

In using the scale described above, it is most important to recognize that individuals, families, and social and cultural groupings will not necessarily include the same traits on a list of masculinity items. As a consequence it is very unfair and often detrimental for a boy to be evaluated in terms of a way of life to which he does not subscribe. The immigrant boy from Thailand is not going to know how to play football. Some parents insist that their children concentrate on playing a musical instrument. The Amish prescribe a way of dressing that most American boys and girls do not follow. Even climbing trees is unknown to the son of a desert nomad. All groups have an idea of masculinity but the diversity in the different interpretations is great.

In the same manner as that developed for males, females can be rated on a scale of femininity by creating a list of traits that apply to females and thinking in terms of the possession of them in the greatest amount as the Most Feminine end of the line and the absence or small quantity as the Least Feminine end, as shown in the figure below.

Scale of Femininity
MOST --LEAST

As with males, it is improbable that any girl will have the maximum of all the traits or even of any single one; nor is it likely that any one will not have the trait at all. Again each girl can be located some place along the line for any trait or combination thereof. A "tomboy" is a girl who climbs trees when people think that is an unfeminine trait.

It should not be assumed that the Least end of the masculine rating scale is related in any way to the feminine scale. A boy who shows up as not very masculine is not necessarily feminine in any way. This would only be the case if the same traits appear on both lists. There are some traits that are only applicable to one sex or the other; some are not sex linked at all, and many will change in how they are evaluated with the passage of time. For example, the location on the masculinity scale of males wearing earrings and necklaces has changed for many, and the same is true of girls wearing pants and jeans. Many fads and fashions change rapidly in time but can still be considered important in any assessment of masculine or feminine. One final caution is in order; namely, it does not follow that a male must be masculine to be normal or typical. Masculinity and femininity are ways of acting, thinking, feeling - a reflection of their sexuality development at a particular stage of their life in a particular setting.

ABOUT SEXUAL IDENTITY

Sexual identity is a term used here to refer to both the awareness of, and convictions about, being a male or a female that are held by a person about himself or herself respectively. This sexual identity as a male or female begins with the learning process at birth and continues for the rest of one's life. It is not identical with the physical characteristics of members of the two sexes although there is a continuing relationship between the development of physical and the overall conception. While there are some similarities in the way male children and female children are reared, there are many differences. Manner of dress, names used to speak to the child, toys provided, even the attitude toward each new behavior acquired by the baby, may be viewed and treated differently. The first few months normally find a pattern established and it will be expanded upon for the next several years. In the next few pages of this chapter, the importance of this early period in a child's life will be elaborated upon because it helps determine one's own definition of who one is and what one can become.

People who live with, work with, and guide young children should be able to answer the following questions:

1. How do infants and young children acquire their sexual identity and their sex role behaviors?

2. What are the most important factors that contribute to this sexual identification process?

3. How can the child be assisted in acquiring a stable and appropriate sexual identity?

A widely used term to cover the factors involved in the answers to these questions is socialization. Socialization encompasses the ways a child learns and the ways one is taught to behave in a group or social situation. The ways infants and young children incorporate attitudes and behaviors must be considered acceptable by parents, siblings, peers, teachers, and "significant others" with whom they interact. "Significant others" are the most important among the people who have contact with a person. They have the most influence so their comments and suggestions are more likely to be followed. It should be noted that which "others" are more significant for the child is strictly judgmental. It is often hard to understand why a child responds to one person and not to another. Furthermore, this is a dynamic phenomenon which changes over time, sometimes quite rapidly. It also changes with the situation, so that a person is a "significant other" at one moment and not at another. In fact the whole socialization process is continuously changing as it develops throughout one's lifetime. As it becomes necessary to relate to others within a changing environment, the definition of "Who am I?" and "What am I?" must inevitably change to fit the moment. As we grow older, we have more and more experience on which to draw in seeking answers for ourselves and our positions in relation to others, but the infant and small child are very limited in this regard. For most young persons, decisions early in life must be made in a very sheltered environment, with a limited number of concerned persons to help. These decisions are critical for determining the direction one's life may take, but they occur mostly in the home, neighborhood, and preschool so that parents, siblings, neighbors, and teachers become the most influential in developing the sexual identity of the child.

Human beings are identified as being either male or female. As individuals, we identify ourselves and are identified by others as belonging to one of the two sexes and our experiences from early infancy on through death are colored by this identification. An individual who engages in heterosexual, homosexual, or bisexual behavior is nevertheless a male or female. This is just as true of the transsexual and the transvestite. In daily life, there are numerous documents, applications, and other situations where a sexual classification is required so the whole idea of a sexual identification is a practical necessity in society.

In her book, <u>Sexual Identity</u>, Betty Yorburg (1974) defines sexual identity as the image of the self as a male or female plus the attitudes and beliefs about what being a member of a particular sex rather than another means. The author believes that this is gradually built up from birth through early childhood. As the child is acquiring the appropriate sexual identity, learning to think, act, and feel by virtue of the fact that he is male (or female if that is the case) is taking place. When a child is given a name by the parents, a form of sexual identity is established. The further development of a sexual identity involves both overt and covert patterns employed by the parents in the manner in which they dress the child, the toys they provide, and the types of discipline and routines established in the home. It is also very significant for the child's self-identification to observe the ways in which the father, as a male, behaves, and the mother, as a female, behaves. These family influences are an integral part of the young child's process of strengthening a conception of himself or herself, of establishing a definition of the human body, and creating an awareness of what males and females are, what they can do, and how they are related to each other. Some writers now suggest new approaches to gender to recognize such categories as masculine, female homosexuals, and feminine, male transvestites (Williams, 1987).

Adam

Toward the end of a parent-teacher conference, Mrs. Kay related the following incident to Adam's parents. During the creative-arts period in kindergarten, the children were making valentines for their mothers, using red paper and printing "I Love You" on them. Several little girls asked for more paper and began to make another valentine just like the first one. Later, on the playground, Mrs. Kay noticed that these children were all giving their second valentine to Adam, each one at a different time. The boy stopped whatever he was doing each time, acknowledged the gift, and talked with each of the givers.

The teacher then commented to Adam's father, Mr. Allen, that she was especially happy to meet him because his son often talked about him, what a nice person he was, what a great golfer he was, and how he talked to Adam about many different things. She noted that Adam was the only kindergarten child invited to join the playground soccer game, and said that he coped quite well with the older boys in the game. However he did become very frustrated when his best friend managed to beat him at racquetball. Mrs. Kay also told the proud parents that

Adam was always kind to an unhappy child and related well to all the children and adults in the school. She commented that Adam was quite masculine in his behavior but she recently noticed him putting on some of the feminine "dress-up" clothes on the playground. She said he looked at himself in the mirror, said he didn't like looking like a girl because he was a boy and wanted to grow up and be like his Daddy.

The teacher then asked Mr. and Mrs. Allen if they would like any additional information about the school or its program, or if they wished to discuss anything with her about Adam. The mother commented that the Safety Awareness Program being conducted in the kindergarten was having quite an impact on the children. One day Mrs. Allen said she was held up in a traffic jam and was late getting home. Adam was waiting for her on a neighbor's porch. He told her that when he came home from school, her car wasn't there and there was a strange man on the front steps. Adam said that Mrs. Kay had warned them to be aware of unusual situations like this and what to do about them. He told his mother that "I just went next door and waited until one of my parents came home."

Mrs. Allen then said, "I would like an honest reaction from you. We may have said too much last night to Adam and gone into too much detail." Mrs. Kay said, "Knowing Adam, that seems unlikely. Tell me what happened." The mother related that they were having a discussion about the baby that was expected in the near future, more specifically about the sex of the child-to-be. They told Adam that it was possible to find out whether he was going to have a brother or a sister but that they preferred to wait until the child was born to find out. Adam said, unexpectedly, "Daddy, I know I look like you but I grew from an egg inside Mommy until I was born. Did you help me start to grow?" Mrs. Kay said that it was an interesting question, what was the response? Mr. Allen said that he answered, "Yes, the sperm from my body united with the egg in your mother's body and then you started to become a baby." Mr. Allen added that he thought he had answered the question very well, but Adam then asked how the sperm got into Mommy's body. The teacher commented that "Adam is a very thoughtful little boy and I hope you gave him a helpful answer."

Mr. Allen said, "This is what I told him and you can be
the judge. I explained that Mother and I hold each other
close and I put my penis inside her vagina, which is an
opening in her body. The sperm comes from my penis and
meets the egg and joins with it and starts growing inside
her body." Mrs. Kay said that he had given a reasonably
simple but honest answer to a very difficult question and
that a six year old as alert as Adam should have grasped it
quite successfully. Adam is an example of a young child
with a strong self-concept who is emotionally mature and
has a strong and well-developed sexuality for his age. He
has a good relationship with his parents and a reasonable
perspective on adult attitudes and behaviors. There is a
realistic sex identity and sense of sex roles with a normal
degree of curiosity and interest about reproduction and
matters pertaining to sex. Perhaps the most significant
aspect of his sexual maturity is his ability to relate to
others, male and female, children and adults. The impact
of intelligent and knowledgeable parents upon Adam is an
integral part of his sexual maturity and establishes the
base upon which others, including peer groups, can build
in the future. Having a father <u>and</u> mother, having a
teacher who is sensitive to his capabilities, being
communicated with in a sound manner, are assets that
not all children have. Our society has not yet found a way
to compensate for the gaps in the learning environment of
many children but the parents and the teachers of young
children are usually the keys and must utilize whatever
strengths they have.

The overall impact of the process of sexual identity becomes apparent
when we realize that the sex of a child cannot be determined by any
behaviors for an indefinite period after birth. There are no arm or leg or
other baby movements that can be identified by sex. Female children are
more physically mature early in infancy, and conversely, male children
are more likely to need medical assistance. One study indicated that
mothers tend to smile and talk more to daughters. The suggested
explanation was that the girls are more mature and therefore respond
more to sensory stimulation. Galinsky, & David (1988, p. 153) write,
"Research shows that during the first year of life sons receive more
physical stimulation and gross motor play, especially from their
fathers, than do daughters. The results are inclusive as to whether
daughters receive more verbal stimulation. There are no sex differences
in smiling and touching and other forms of social interaction between
parents and their infant boys and girls." There is much interest as to the
actual amount and kinds of influence those who care for the young child

have upon the growth and development of that child. Parents and others are immediately informed of the sex affiliation of the child and it appears this affects their actions toward the baby from the beginning. It seems beautiful eyes or sturdy shoulders are in the eyes of the beholder when the child's sex is known. There is no question however, that the child must learn what being one particular sex means and what must be done. The options are many and the flexibility of the human child to follow one path rather than another is almost unlimited, so while the sex is given, the behavior that goes with it is not.

SOME VARIATIONS IN SEXUAL IDENTITY

In 1966, the first gender identity clinic was started at Johns Hopkins University Hospital in Baltimore, Maryland. There are now a number of these clinics in operation in the United States, and several other countries. These clinics function through a team of specialists representing a number of disciplines including psychology, sociology, genetics, endocrinology, embryology, and medicine. Numerous aspects of scientific research and theory are incorporated into the program to study and treat problems of sexual differentiation and to investigate human sexuality in depth.

Children with defects in their sex organs are studied in the Psychohormonal Research Unit at Johns Hopkins. Homosexuals, bisexuals, transsexuals, and transvestites are also studied and treated. It is through the work and research being done in these areas that a fuller understanding of the two sexes, the differences and similarities between them, and aberrations - as well as the range of behavior - is being studied. Although a great deal of this research does not deal directly with young children, it can be anticipated that as additional knowledge is gained, a better grasp of development at various ages will be acquired, with the opportunity to encourage or discourage behaviors that are found desirable or undesirable by agreed upon standards.

Some writers contend that homosexuality, transsexuality, and transvestite behaviors are psychosexual in nature when manifested in daily life (Money and Tucker, 1975). They also claim that such behaviors originate after birth or infancy with no physiological determinants. It is proposed by some that some children are born with a pre-disposition toward these sexual identity statuses. There are currently no satisfactory laboratory tests to establish the presence or absence of any distinct genetic, hormonal, or anatomical patterns common to these areas.

Birth Defects

A number of children are born who have some disorder among their many biological sex traits. In rare instances, an external examination does not reveal the child's sex category but there are tests available to determine whether a newborn baby is male or female in terms of its chromosomal pattern. In the past, the physician would arbitrarily identify the child as being of one particular sex on the birth certificate, or even let the parents express their preference and accept that. Today it is often recommended that a name that could be applied to a child of either sex be assigned while the biological sex is being determined. In some cases, surgery to reconstruct the sex defect is clearly identifiable and relatively easily carried out. In others it is a long drawn out series of surgeries and reconstructions, with an accompanying concern for the psychological problems that may occur.

There seems to be almost no limit to the kinds of defects that are present at birth. An infant may be born with both ovaries and testes, or with external genitalia so ambiguous as to make sex determination impossible. In other instances, the genitalia are quite severely deformed, such as a hard lump of skin for a penis. The following case is an extreme one which illustrates both the extent of the problems that can happen and the strength of the family and child in coping with it. This report is summarized from a written report prepared by the mother for the teacher so she could help the child adjust to the class room situation as it became necessary.

Francis

Because of major problems at birth and a series of major operations, Francis' first exposure to a large group of children was when he entered kindergarten at age five. The teacher did not initially identify any problems, other than the presence of a hearing aid, because Francis was a delightful child, extremely intelligent, happy, and cooperative in the group. At the beginning of the school year, he encountered a few problems with his peers but quickly learned to be more cooperative and adjust to his frustrations. He also related well to adults and revealed a very positive self image that allowed him to resolve his problems. After two weeks, the mother came to school to explain his medical history and how the parents, with the help of educational and medical experts, had worked to help the little boy.

At birth, the parents were informed that they had a girl, but were advised shortly that the baby would be labeled a girl pending further examinations and tests. A few hours after birth, Francis was operated upon to make an incision to create a rectal opening. After a week of genetic and chromosomal testing, the child was established as a male but with more surgery ahead. When he was brought home after a week, under his diaper he resembled a girl except for a micro penis near the rectum.

At age one, surgery was undertaken to repair the first of the birth defects. The first step was to transplant the penis to its proper location. Francis then received a series of sixteen hormone shots to enlarge the penis, which would reduce scarring, permit additional surgery, and make the penis more functional in later years. A urethra, or canal from the bladder to the penal opening was constructed, put in place, and then an operation to close the area next to the rectum was performed. Surgery was required several more times on the penis because of breaks which permitted the discharge of urine in several places. Another operation was performed to bring down the testicles after a series of hormone shots failed to do so. At the time of entering school, Francis had had ten operations on his genitals with one opening still present so further surgery was to be done.

In addition to the defects in the genital and rectal areas, Francis was almost completely deaf at birth, had a heart murmur, requiring a catheterization at six weeks of age, currently has a great deal of scar tissue, but is progressing relatively normally in kindergarten. No explanation has been given for the birth defects, but the doctors said they knew of no reason why another child would have any problems. The parents are anxious to have another child but feel they are most fortunate to have had Francis. The mother's report was concluded with the following statement, "If Francis can not have normal sexual relations when he is an adult, my husband and I hope and pray he will find someone who will love and marry him for all of his other good qualities." The teacher commented that Francis has a very healthy sexuality and that the parents obviously played a major part.

The multiple problems of Francis and his apparently good adjustment to them indicates the flexibility of the human being in coping when the support is present at home. The utilization of professional assistance throughout childhood and the love and affection of the parents combined to make the child accept his life as a relatively normal one. If this child can find similar support from teachers, peers, and "significant others," as well as his parents, the odds of a rewarding and pleasant life are very good. The following case is an illustration of another side of coping with birth defects when they occur.

Andy

> Andy was born with a defective opening in his penis. Reconstructive surgery was not undertaken until he was three years of age. At this time the surgeon told the parents the condition was corrected and the child would have no further problems, either physical or emotional. Unfortunately this did not turn out to be true, as Andy still revealed considerable trauma in nursery school. The teacher discovered this when Andy became hysterical because another youngster opened the bathroom door while he was urinating. When the teacher informed the mother about the incident, the mother told her of the operation and its effect upon Andy's emotional character. She said her son refused to let anyone, except her, see him nude and would not let anyone see him urinate. She added that, despite her efforts to help him, he repeatedly stated that he hated his penis, that it was bad, and that he would like to cut it off. The mother said she believed the surgeon had been sincere, but wished he had been more perceptive and helpful after the operation. She felt this would have enabled her to prevent the severe emotional and psychological problems that had developed.

In the case of Francis, the medical staff, the parents, and the teacher were continually working to meet the needs of the child by communicating with each other and the boy. In the case of Andy, the relation between the doctor and the parents was not satisfactory, as it turned out. Furthermore, the parents did not advise the teacher of the situation until a problem arose. It is not necessary or our intent to suggest that anyone was wrong or right in either case, but to point out the positive consequences of communication among all those concerned as well as the power of love, affection, and understanding on the part of the parents.

Homosexual and Bisexual Behavior

An important need for a young child today is to learn to understand, enjoy, and appreciate one's own sexuality and to respect that of other people, in spite of differences that may exist. In the known history of human behavior heterosexual relationships have been most commonly accepted, as well as being most prevalent, but homosexual and bisexual relationships have existed as well. Most parents expect their children to be heterosexual as adults and often have difficulty understanding why any child might turn in a different direction.

People become homosexual or bisexual for reasons that are not fully understood at the present time. The theories that are directed toward explaining these behaviors are generally based on biological factors or socio-cultural explanations (Gagnon, 1977). The basic problem with finding causes for particular kinds of human behavior is that they cannot be created under controlled conditions in a laboratory but must be studied under the everyday circumstances in which they actually occur. This means that the existence of homosexual preferences is not usually known until a person is grown, often a teenager or older, so that the circumstances of his ancestry and rearing patterns can only be recalled and interpreted, not observed as they occurred.

Homosexuals are persons who seek sexual satisfaction from people of the same sex rather than the opposite sex. The terms "lesbian" and "gay" have been applied to female and male homosexuals, respectively. It is estimated that five to ten per cent of males and three to five per cent of females are exclusively homosexual. An additional number are oriented toward homosexual preferences but are also heterosexual to some extent. In the last few decades there has been greater awareness and acceptance of homosexuality and bisexuality. Civil rights groups, women's liberation groups, and the Gay Liberation Movement have aided the publicity given homosexuality and have also urged that all kinds of laws which are directed toward homosexuality be removed.

Recent research on homosexual behavior and its causes has moved away from some of the widely held beliefs of earlier years. Evidence does not support the view that a strong mother and a weak father is likely to cause the male child to be homosexual. On the other hand, allowing a boy to behave in a feminine manner and dress in girl's clothing without being discouraged may have some impact. These behaviors, combined with a rejection of rough and tumble play, may cause an isolation from the male environment. Many homosexuals do have heterosexual experiences but do not find them satisfying. There is some evidence that sex preferences as a part of one's sexuality is established fairly early in life and is not really a matter of choice. In fact it is suggested by some, that therapists should not attempt to modify or change homosexuality but should help the person develop more positive feelings about his sexual direction.

A recent study by Richard Green, a psychiatrist, (1987) found that young boys who persistently acted like girls were very likely to become homosexual or bisexual in their adult lives. The findings revealed that neither therapy designed to discourage the extremely feminine behavior nor ideal child-rearing activities could guarantee that the boys would develop as heterosexuals. Green and others think the findings indicate that some children have an innate "receptivity" to environmental factors that encourage a homosexual orientation. Whether such a predisposition is genetic or the result of prenatal influences, or a combination, is unknown. Green believes that homosexuality may well be a result of the interaction of cultural, parental, and genetic factors.

The coming generation will likely find more freedom to pursue their sexual lives as they see fit. When today's young children reach adolescence and adulthood, they will likely find more acceptance of any homosexual or bisexual tendencies than is true now. Teachers and parents however, have a new and difficult set of responsibilities due to the growing openness about homosexuality and bisexuality. It is necessary that they be knowledgeable about these types of behavior. They must realize that sexual preferences do not necessarily affect other areas of human behavior. There are some feminine-behaving males who are fully heterosexual and females who are masculine acting and feminine in orientation. It is not accurate to judge a person's sexual preference by manner of speech, dress, or personal mannerisms. Regardless of sexual orientation, all persons need love, acceptance, companionship, success, work, fun, home, and friends, among other things.

While accepting the importance of an awareness that sexual choices are not the basis for other kinds of behaviors, parents and teachers must consider the advantages of guiding their children toward heterosexuality at the present time. Perhaps the major justification is that it will reduce the number of adjustments that will have to be made in later years. Social adjustments are often difficult for the homosexual, in spite of their increasing acceptance, because those who do not accept them can create severe problems. When the latter are in positions of responsibility, they can prevent promotions, advances in pay, transfers, and similar benefits. It is also true that threats of exposure to others or widespread publicity are difficult for some homosexuals to cope with. This can also have impact on those around them, including members of the family.

Judi

Judi lived with her mother and her mother's lesbian lover. The mother was attending a university and the school newspaper wrote a lengthy article about the relationship including some graphic details about their sexual activities. The story was then picked up and reprinted in several local newspapers. This was followed by a number of letters to the editors. One of the unfortunate consequences was that Judi began to be ostracized by others in the kindergarten class because their mothers told them not to play with the girl because her mother was "bad." The teacher was able to minimize the situation in school when she became aware of it, but the situation continued on the playground and in the neighborhood.

There is increasing acceptance that there is a significant physiological component in the determination of one's sexual identity. The parents play an important role but they cannot necessarily prevent a child from becoming a homosexual so it may be most important as to the ways in which they accept it. It is common for the relationship between heterosexual parents and homosexual children to be strained and result in partial or total separation unless some resolution can be found. Constructive actions include the following:

1. A parent should observe if a child exhibits opposite-sex types of behavior and not be indifferent to it.

2. When a young child persistently dresses up like a person of the opposite sex, the parents should neither encourage it or show any type of approval.

3. The parents should encourage a child to overcome any dislike of activities that only boys or girls normally engage in, and encourage him or her toward a fuller participation in heterosexual activities.

Bisexuality has not been studied as thoroughly as homosexual behavior but it is known that bisexuals generally lean toward heterosexual activities with some homosexual experiences in addition. Sometimes the homosexual contacts occur prior to marriage and are not repeated in later years. The reverse of this situation does occur but is not common.

Awareness of bisexuality has increased considerably in recent years; a number of prominent persons in sports, entertainment, and business have admitted to such behavior, and it is then further publicized through the media. On the surface, homosexuals and bisexuals appear to be better adjusted, more accepting, and more satisfied than in the past but the depth of these feelings is not easily determined. Some students of sexuality believe that bisexual feelings emerge later than homosexual ones and are more closely tied to learning and social experiences than to biological ones. According to the Kinsey Institute, bisexuality is practiced by about sixteen percent of all males and nine percent of all females. One evidence of the increased awareness and acceptance of bisexuality is the emergence of colloquialisms in the language, e.g., on the fence, AC-DC, going both ways, and switch hitters; these sometimes appear in comedians' routines and even in children's conversations. These linguistic additions are sometimes used negatively, but they also represent a knowledge of bisexuality, and in the long run, a diminution of negativism, rejection, or guilt feelings.

Gagnon (1977) believes that in our freer sexual atmosphere today, bisexuality is increasingly recognized as a distinct option by both homosexual and heterosexual practitioners. Margaret Mead (1975) has suggested that it was time to recognize bisexuality as a normal form of sexual behavior. She added that the recognition of bisexuality in one's self and in others is part of the whole 20th century movement to accord to each individual - regardless of race, class, nationality, age, or sex - the right to be a person who has a social identity that is worthy of dignity and respect.

Bisexuals often encounter problems in their relationships with others but also tend to receive some understanding and acceptance. In actuality, every adult human being is capable of bisexual behavior and it is possible that most have fantasized at one time or another about being bisexual in some way. Gagnon (1977) also points to a problem that is unique for bisexuals when he notes that in a world where there is competition for sex, love, and intimacy, heterosexuals usually have only competition with other heterosexuals, and homosexuals from other homosexuals. But for a bisexual, both homosexuals and heterosexuals represent a threat which does not add to a bisexual's sense of security.

Transsexuals

Transsexuals want to be, or believe they are, of the opposite sex rather than the one defined by their biological, anatomical, and chromosomal characteristics. Physiologically they are of one sex, but psychologically they are of the other. The roots of this incongruity are not known but to the persons so affected it is a very real situation. This is a different condition from the strong desire of some males and females who wish they were of the opposite sex. Many people have such feelings occasionally, or perhaps frequently, usually in relation to situations where they believe there would be an advantage or a pleasant response if they were something different. Transsexuals should not be confused with homosexuals, who have a personal and sexual preference for persons of the same sex, but which is not translated into a desire to be of that sex. Transsexuals, in their associations with persons of the opposite sex, intensely desire to be of that other sex and, in essence, identify themselves as such. In contrast, Grimm (1987) writes that homosexuals seem highly sensitive to the cultural meanings behind the concept of their own gender.

Transsexuals, in general, experience a great deal of dissatisfaction and unhappiness with their situation, and frequently require extensive counselling. In some instances, they seek hormone therapy and sex change surgery. The hormone therapy is undertaken for a year or more while the person strives to dress and behave as one of the opposite sex before the operation is actually performed. In later years, some of these persons marry, often with success, and are able to achieve satisfactory sex relations with their partners. While it is not possible to become a parent in the biological sense, many do adopt a child or two and succeed as parents very well.

Transsexuality does not exist with regard to young children, at least on a conscious level. Adults can rarely remember their pre-school years, except for isolated incidents. They talk about things they said and did but usually this comes from being told by parents and others, not from recall. Two things are clear, though: many homosexuals claim they were uncomfortable with the opposite sex when they were young, and many transsexuals state they can not remember when they did not desire to be of the opposite sex. Basically transsexuality cannot be detected or predicted at an early age. Working to create a healthy sexuality is all that can be done and at such time as non-heterosexual behavior begins to become evident, professional help and guidance is needed.

Transvestites

A transvestite is a person, usually a male, who has a strong desire to dress in clothes associated with the opposite sex. This practice is known as cross-dressing, and may be related to sexual satisfaction. Money and Tucker (1975) state that gender-identity clinic specialists are discovering that a true transvestite has a two-part identity. When he is dressed as a male, which he is biologically, he acts like a male and desires to maintain his penis even though he also has a strong urge to dress in female clothes. A transvestite who is also homosexual has male sex partners and is aware of his maleness regardless of his attire. A transvestite who is not homosexual usually marries, may have children, but will retain the urge to dress up in women's clothes.

Some transvestites change their sexual-identity when they put on female garments and assume a female personality by adopting a different name and a different manner of walking, talking, and a set of mannerisms that he believes appropriate for his female personality. In a few states it is illegal to engage in cross-dressing but such laws are rarely enforced. The male transvestites who have been studied have consistently been found to be physically normal males so the explanation does not seem to be a biological one.

Children, starting at an early age, enjoy dressing up in the clothes of adults, including those of the opposite sex, and often attempt to adopt some of the mannerisms they think are appropriate. This type of dramatic play involves taking the role of others and is a normal and healthy part of growing up. However, it is important for parents and teachers to take careful note of any child who seems to feel a strong compulsion to dress up in such a manner; especially they should be aware of any child who begins to distort his actual sex with that associated with the type of clothes worn. Such behavior is sometimes associated with conflicting parental demands and may result in psychological problems if the conflicts are not resolved. However, dressing up behavior by young children, unless compulsive, does not seem to have any relationship to transvestism in later years. The existence of transvestite behavior by parents is often not known by children. Some wives are unaware of their husband's activities and others are able to accept it in stride, especially if the marriage is successful and reasonably happy. If a child does happen to discover a father's dressing up, it needs to be explained as a private activity that does not really have any importance.

Brian

In a summer day care program, a lot of the time is spent on the playground. One of the teachers, with almost fifty children ranging in age from four to twelve, decided to take several boxes of dress-up clothes to help entertain them. The clothes included items for both sexes and the children were free to pick and choose as they pleased. Normally, the girls spent more time than the boys using the dress-up clothes in dramatic play. The girls engaged in such role playing as mothers, teenagers, and teachers. They also played creatively in a variety of other roles. For example, when wearing a black and red cape they become Batman, king, magician, prince, or the Devil. The boys also played with the cape and being Batman or some Superman type was the favorite role. The boys usually preferred masculine clothes, e.g., a flyer's helmet with an oxygen mask as a favorite item. It was also common for the boys to dress up in women's clothes and prance around for a short time. They would laugh and joke and tease each other and then go on to other activities.

Four year old Brian did not follow this pattern however. He did not want to play with anything but the female clothing. As soon as he got to the playground he would go to the boxes of clothes and choose the prettiest and most feminine items, including jewelry and high heeled shoes. Brian was somewhat effeminate in his actions but, when he got dressed in women's attire, he successfully mimicked a girl in mannerism, walk, and speech. Brian enjoyed acting in this manner, paid little or no attention to what the other children were doing, and also ignored the teasing. He continued in these behaviors for the entire period the children were on the playground.

One day Brian said to the supervising teacher, "When I grow up I am going to be a mommy and have a baby." Mrs. Kirk replied, "No Brian, you will be a father because you are a boy and when you are a man, you can not have a baby." Brian replied angrily, "I am not a boy, I am a girl, and I will be a mommy and have babies in my stomach." Mrs. Kirk repeated that he was a boy and attempted to get him to wear male's clothing as well as that of females, with no real success.

Every day Brian would ask the teachers if they were going outside and play with the clothes. He was quite compulsive about wearing them and became angry if he could not have the right ones. He even asked the teacher to take the clothes he preferred away from the other children. Because of Brian's behavior, and also the fact that the other children were responding negatively, calling him "sissy" and making fun of him, Mrs. Kirk decided to stop providing the dress-up clothes for a while. She also discussed Brian's compulsion with women's clothing with his mother, and also his contention that he was a girl. She recommended that the two work together to reinforce the idea that he was a boy and avoid dressing-up activities. She also suggested seeking professional help if Brian continued to have difficulty in developing a realistic sexual identity and the appropriate sex-role behaviors.

Roy

During a share and tell period in kindergarten, Roy said that something funny happened to him at home last night. He said that his mother had gone out and his Daddy stayed home with him. Then he added, "I woke up after I'd been asleep for a while and went to find Daddy because I was scared. I found him in his bedroom and he was wearing Mother's underwear and her wig and looking at himself in the mirror. Daddy sure looked funny when he saw me but when I laughed he got mad and said I would be punished if I told Mommy."

The teacher quickly changed the subject but the incidents that followed were more difficult to cope with. She received two calls that evening. The first, from Roy's mother who wanted to know exactly what had happened at school. The teacher told the mother what Roy had said and added that young children have vivid imaginations. The mother thanked her and indicated that if she found the event was true, she and her husband would seek professional help.

The second call was from the mother of Larry, another child in the class, who wanted to know if Larry's report to her about Roy's story was true. She said she was concerned because her son played at Roy's house a lot and she might want to stop it. The teacher confirmed the story in general terms and again noted that children have vivid imaginations. The next day Roy told his teacher that he was afraid his parents were going to get a divorce because he told what his daddy did. He said that he wasn't supposed to tell his mother but nothing was said about not telling others. The teacher also heard Larry tell Roy that he couldn't play at his house anymore because his Daddy did bad things. The teacher reassured Roy that his Daddy was not bad, and added that he had done nothing wrong.

It is not difficult to imagine the kinds of problems Brian and Roy are likely to encounter in developing a set of sex roles with which they will be comfortable. Both children are involved in situations that are generally illogical and incompatible in the larger world in which they live and will continue to live. The process of learning to be a male, and the behaviors that go with it, is ongoing and will inevitably involve contradictions that need to be resolved in the child's mind. In most situations, and for most people, transsexuals and transvestites are neither understood nor accepted. The young child who is oriented in such a direction or who encounters it in the early years must ultimately find an explanation that satisfies his or her own needs and is compatible with experiences that they have had and will have. Much depends on the parents and those who will work with the child. If the answers given are unsatisfactory or inadequate, the consequences are apt to involve social maladjustment or psychological confusion or both.

THE SEXUAL IDENTITY LEARNING PROCESS

Agents of socialization such as parents, siblings, teachers, and peers, either through direct instruction or by example, do communicate to the infant and young child those attitudes and behaviors that are considered appropriate for each sex. In many family situations, the child is exposed to two parents, one of each sex, who can serve as role models and reinforce each other in the learning process. One of the interesting questions is the extent to which the same sex parent and the opposite sex parent influence their children of the same and opposite sex. Rearing children involves a very complex set of relationships which have not fully been analyzed by researchers from the many disciplines which have a relevance for the matter. Maccoby and Jacklin (1974, p. 1-2) offer three major psychological theories as the "hows" and "whys" of sex differentiation:

1. Through imitation - children choose same sex models for patterning their own behavior. This selective modeling need not be conscious on the child's part.

2. Through praise and encouragement - parents (and others) reward and praise boys for what they conceive to be "boy-like" behavior and actively discourage boys when they engage in activities that are considered feminine; similarly, girls receive positive reinforcement for "feminine" behavior, and negative reinforcement for "masculine" behavior.

3. Through self-socialization - the child first develops a concept of what it is to be male or female, then as one gains more understanding of his or her own sex identity, attempts are made to fit behavior in a given situation with what is believed appropriate."

Studies over the years have reinforced what seemed obvious, that sex role learning begins early in life with the parents as the primary influence. This early research also suggested that in families where the father is absent, the male child is slower to develop male sex role traits than he is in families where the father is present. The finding is based essentially on the fact that the boy has no male to model after.

Carl

Carl was a fatherless child at the time he entered kindergarten and, in fact, had had very little contact with any males during his first five years. He needed help and encouragement from the teacher, Mrs. Ekstrom, to enable him to play with other children, especially the boys. For several weeks, Carl was shy, frightened, and hesitated to enter any play activities. He either sat and watched or played alone with a toy. Gradually he began to play with girls at the table activities but always stopped and went near the teacher if boys came to the table. Carl avoided all communication and other interaction with boys in the class and hid behind the piano if a male entered the room. He entered none of the dramatic play activities and stood near the teacher on the playground. He did talk freely with his teacher, apparently feeling secure only when he was near her.

Carl lived in a home with his mother, two grandmothers, and six sisters. No father nor other male visited in the home. Although Carl did not wear dresses, he did wear clothing that was handed down from his sisters. As the youngest, he was overprotected by his sisters who were the only children he had much chance to play with.

The teacher had had one of the sisters in school and had good rapport with the mother. She requested a conference with the mother after three weeks of school, when she described Carl's behavior to the mother. The mother indicated an awareness of it and said she hoped that playing with the other boys in kindergarten would change him. She added that part of the situation was probably caused by a traumatic experience the year before when some older boys held him close to a bonfire and threatened to throw him in. Since that time he had been scared of all males and suffered from nightmares. Mrs. Ekstrom assured the mother that she would help and also suggested that Carl be given more responsibility in the home and the opportunity to do more things for himself and by himself.

After giving the boy time to adjust to school and to develop a trust of her, Mrs. Ekstrom began to take steps to help. First, she joined him occasionally in his play. Then she asked Anne, whom he seemed to like, to play with them and enter into some dramatic play together. One day the teacher and Carl needed a third person to operate a manipulative toy and she casually asked Mike to help them and the play continued. A few days later, she arranged for Anne and Mike to work together and then asked Carl to join them and help build with the small blocks. It was very difficult for Carl but he gradually became less fearful and achieved some self-confidence. The teacher made sure he did not get involved in situations where he might become frightened.

Carl continued to hide behind the piano when a male entered the room, until the day a sky-diver visited the classroom. He was dressed in his sky-diving outfit and ultimately invited the children to try on his helmet. Carl left his refuge to try it on. During the afternoon, Carl gradually began to ask the skydiver questions. After that occurrence, Carl did not retreat to his hiding place but remained near Mrs. Ekstrom when males appeared. Several months later a male Health and Physical Education teacher began once-a-week sessions with the class. He gave Carl some special attention, won his confidence, and became a strong role model for the child. By the end of the year, Carl was interacting freely with males in the school environment.

The mother and sisters were creating more contacts with men in the home and the neighborhood. At the last conference of the year, the mother said she was most pleased with the changes in Carl, that his nightmares were gone, and he seemed quite secure. At the beginning of school, Carl was unable to develop a sexual identity as a male or to achieve a masculine type of sexuality because he had too many negative forces at work. Before he reached the age of six, he had a traumatic experience involving males; he never had a significant male role-model either inside or outside the home; he had learned to be comfortable playing with girls and utilizing their kinds of toys and games; he had acquired some feminine mannerisms, emphasized by his small stature and delicate features, and he had experienced cross-dressing by wearing his sister's clothes. The influences mentioned do not indicate the probability of the boy becoming transsexual or a transvestite but they would be somewhat other than normal for a boy his age. By honest communication between mother and teacher, the negative forces were reduced and controlled while Carl is still quite young. He is interacting with males and becoming aware of himself and the role he can play within socially acceptable limits. While he may still encounter difficulties under pressure, he is receiving help within a framework of love and concern by others.

Researchers generally accept the view that sexual identity is learned rather than genetically determined. This indicates that life experiences determine whether the individual sees himself as and acts like a "normal" male or something else, e.g., female, homosexual, transsexual, etc. It is also believed that sexual identity and sex-typed behaviors are established during the first three years of a child's life. Attempts to change sexual identity after the age of two are not recommended because it is very difficult and will likely create serious problems for the future.

HOW DOES THE YOUNG CHILD LEARN ROLE BEHAVIOR?

Behavioral scientists generally concur that parents are and should be the primary socializing agents for the infant and young child and for the acquisition of sexual identity and sex-role behaviors. Parents guide and influence their child's actions through the kinds of love, care, and verbalization they utilize. Most parents spend much time talking with their child long before it can understand or respond. Even infants often hear, "You look like Mommy," (or Daddy); "You are a good little girl" or "You're a bad child"; as well as the frequent "no, no, no," or "stop that."

Through this daily verbal interaction, the child is exposed to information, attitudes, and concepts of appropriate and inappropriate behavior; and most importantly, the child begins to learn "who I am." Children are learning the differences between sexes, the sexual group to which they belong, what sex-role behaviors are appropriate for each at a given age, and whether to accept or reject membership in a designated sex group. Maccoby & Jacklin (1974, p. 365-366) suggest that gender constancy is not necessary in order for self-socialization into sex roles to begin. They write, "Children as young as three achieve rudimentary understanding of their own sex identity, even though their ability to group others according to sex is imperfect and the notions about the permanence of their own sex identity is incomplete. As soon as a boy knows that he is a boy in any sense, he is likely to begin to prefer to do what he believes are boy-like things. Of course he will not selectively imitate male models if he does not yet know which other people around him are in the same sex category as himself. But he will nevertheless try to match his own behavior to his limited concept of what attitudes are sex-appropriate."

Parents should be fully aware their own behavior as role models for their children is important, as is their behavior relating directly to them, to each other, and to other siblings in the family. Parents also provide a wide variety of learning experiences as they care for their child and provide for the needs and growth. The wearing apparel, the assigned chores, and the toys and games provided all affect the child as he or she learns a sexual identity. The kinds of chores, toys, and games are usually indicative of what the parents consider suitable for fostering the child's masculinity or femininity. Whether parents are conscious of it or not, they provide many learning experiences which are very powerful, especially when coupled with love, praise, rewards, and encouragement. Adverse criticism and expressions of disapproval and displeasure also have an impact but are less effective because they do not indicate what is acceptable. Many a little boy has cried because one of his parents called him a "sissy." It is interesting to note that the label "tomboy" for a little girl seems much less traumatic and may even be a source of some pride.

While many young parents are more casual today in their selection of toys and games and may buy dolls for their sons and space ships and rocket guns for their daughters, they still supply many sex-typed things for the children. There is evidence to indicate that some parents deliberately encourage their children to develop sex-typed interests in the games they recommend and teach and the toys they buy. Some parents go further and actively discourage their young sons from play that might be considered feminine, such as wearing high heels or putting on mother's lipstick. This type of play tends to upset many parents more than a little girl's utilization of masculine games or clothes or play roles. This is likely due to the parent's fear that feminine behavior on the part of small boys may be an indication of homosexual tendencies. However masculine behavior by little girls is rarely defined in the same way. Whatever the reasons, parents do emphasize the male child's masculinity in dress and behavior more than they do the female child's femininity in the comparable areas. Perhaps this is a form of male chauvinism that persists but for the present it is rather widespread and has considerable impact on the developing sexuality of the young child.

Although a teacher has less influence than the parents in most cases, some children need the teacher's guidance and support. Boys are normally more in need of role models, as the father is more likely to be the absent parent in one-parent families. While female teachers can not play the father's role, they can assist these children by bringing males in the classroom. This can be accomplished by the use of older children, other teachers, administrators, and non-teaching personnel within the school environment. A male bus driver can be a small boy's friend, available each day. Any such attachment may be strong enough for the child to identify with the person as a sex-role model. Resource people who visit the class not only provide additional interaction for the child, but also add to his understanding of the roles available to males. It is more meaningful to a child to be a policeman in his dramatic play if he has met and talked with one and has a first-hand idea of what a policeman does.

While directing the play activities, the teacher of young children can assist them to interact positively with each other. She can, for example, help those who prefer to play exclusively with one sex to learn how to play with and relate to both sexes. This is important because by age six a child begins to use his peers, his parents, and some adult "significant others" as models. Therefore, a child who is a favorite with other children and a strong leader can help other children identify with him or her and learn their appropriate sex-role behaviors. On the other hand, the timid and insecure child needs a measure of protection while the teacher guides him or her into developing self-confidence in interactions with classmates. A teacher can create situations and use "teachable moments" to accomplish this. If a child can excel and act as a leader on occasion, his or her shyness and lack of self-confidence will gradually diminish. The vignette of Carl in this chapter illustrates a planned procedure to help a child. If a child is rejected, manipulated, called derogatory names, or dominated by a strong leader in group play, the teacher has a responsibility to stop such behavior. An explanation to an individual child or to the group will often suffice. A two or three year old will respond to a "no," while a four, five or six year old requires more discussion about behavior. There are audio-visual learning materials that can help the young child distinguish acceptable from unacceptable behavior. Programs such as Sesame Street sometimes offer opportunities for children to learn from discussing the program and its implications during the program or at a later date. Unless controlled, negative influences on sex-role identifications tend to be negative for the over-all development of a healthy sexuality.

A nursery or kindergarten program should be conducive to learning sexual identity and sex-role behaviors, within an environment designed to enable each child to find recognition and have experiences that foster a positive self-image. Structured learning activities, literature, art, music, social studies, trips, resource persons, school personnel, and parents all contribute to the child's acquisition of a sexual identity. The teacher has the responsibility for helping each child learn who he or she is, and more importantly, to feel good about himself or herself. Every child needs to feel like an accepted member of the peer group who relates well to both sexes and identifies with one's own sex.

Most children do not encounter any major difficulty in recognizing and accepting their sexual identity. Various backgrounds and previous experiences may contribute to many minor adjustment problems along the way. Some children are reared in institutional settings rather than private homes; some experience only one parent homes; and still others, who have both parents present, may nevertheless lack an adequate sex-role model. These are the types of children who are likely to benefit most in the school environment from any strong models with whom they can interact and who can help them recognize and accept their sexual identity. However, the complexity of this need and its achievement should not be minimized.

Susie

Early in the year, Susie's kindergarten teacher realized the little girl thought she was a boy. She always referred to herself as a boy and adopted the male role in all dramatic play activities. She became very angry when other children told her she was a girl, not a boy. She shouted, "I am a boy! Why don't you believe me?" During the first parent-teacher conference after school began, the teacher asked the parents if they were concerned that Susie thought she was a boy. The parents admitted they were quite concerned because they thought the little girl would stop pretending to be a boy after school started. They said they realized now that she was not pretending and often claimed she could do many activities at school better than any of the girls because she was a boy. The mother added that she refused to wear any of her girl's clothes, both under- and outer garments.

The parents then volunteered the information that perhaps they had created the situation of Susie's self-deception. It was explained that they had a young son who died under tragic circumstances when Susie was only a week old. The mother said that she had continually referred to Susie as her little boy and called her Jimmy for the next two years. She said she felt this unusual adjustment had kept her from a nervous breakdown or complete collapse. The father added that he was generally aware of what was happening but that he didn't consider it significant because he was so concerned with his wife's health and his own grief from the death.

The teacher was told that Susie wore all of her deceased brother's clothing until she was two years old. The parents said that they rationalized this behavior as being for economic reasons but later realized they were both trying to replace the lost son. They said further that they had not realized until the last few weeks that their previous behavior could be causing serious problems for Susie. They asked the teacher where they could go for professional help and she referred them to the school psychologist who began counselling for both the parents and child.

This is Susie's self-portrait. Susie was asked about her drawing, however, she was not asked to explain the letters. It should be noted that she may have written the word "DAD".

Figure 4-2 Susie's self-portrait

The teacher and school psychologist were with Susie when the psychologist asked Susie to draw a picture of herself. The psychologist then asked the child to describe her drawing. Susie assured them this was a picture of herself and then pointed to and labeled the breasts, naval and penis. Later the psychologist told the teacher that Susie's drawing gave credence to her belief that she was a boy. (that she was confused in her gender identity). (See Figure 4-2)

This counselling continued for the six years Susie was in the elementary school. At the end of this time, the psychologist reported to the teacher that Susie still did not have a healthy sexuality. The little girl had a poor self-concept, she was still masculine in her behavior and appearance, and she claimed during the counselling sessions that she was really a boy but she had to pretend to be a girl. She also avoided interacting with other little girls whenever possible.

Through relationships with other people, the young child gradually moves toward a concept of itself and a recognition of his or her sexual identity and what it means. The strength and adequacy of one's self-concept and the degree of acceptance of that sexual identity are influenced by a variety of people - parents, siblings, relatives, family, friends, store clerks, etc. - but the family members usually play the key role in both aspects of development. The case of Susie reveals the difficulty of even professionally trained personnel being able to overcome a misdirected parental influence. The teacher must be fully cognizant of the power of parents as the child starts to expand his horizons and interact with the teacher and other children. When the young child enters a pre-school or school program, the peer groups begins to be a strong influence in the development of a child's sexuality and increases its importance with each passing year.

QUESTIONS FOR DISCUSSION

1. What factors determine the number and the influence of a young child's "significant others"? When and why do they change?

2. What traits do you believe should be identified as masculine? Which ones are feminine? Rate some people you know from one to ten on each trait and add up their scores and compare the findings.

3. Why does a person working with young children need to know about a child's birth defects, even though they may have been corrected?

4. If a teacher has a child with a homosexual parent, should this have any affect upon the teacher-parent relationship? Explain your answer whether it is yes or no.

5. Can teachers identify potential homosexuals, transsexuals, and transvestite among the young children they work with regularly? If your answer is yes, do you believe any action is called for?

CHAPTER REFERENCES

Gagnon, J. (1977). Human sexualities. Glenview, IL: Scott Foresman.

Galinsky, E. & J. David (1988). The preschool years: family strategy that work - from experts and parents. New York: Time Books.

Green, R. (1987). The "sissy boy syndrome" and the development of homosexuality. New Haven, CN: Yale University Press.

Grimm, D.E. (1987). Toward a theory of gender. American Behavioral Scientist, 31: 66-85.

Leuptow, L. (1984) Adolescent sex roles and social change. New York: Columbia niversity Press.

Maccoby, E. & C. Jacklin (1974). The psychology of sex differences. Stanford, CA: Stanford University Press.

Mead, M. (1975). Bisexuality: what it is all about? Redbook, January, P. 31.

Money, J. & P. Tucker (1975). Sexual signatures: on being a man or being a woman. Boston: Little, Brown and Company.

Williams, W.L. (1987). Women, men, and others. American Behavioral Scientist, 31: 135-141.

Yorburg, B. (1974). Sexual identity. New York: John Wiley and Sons.

CHAPTER V

SEXUAL ABUSE OF YOUNG CHILDREN

THE NATURE OF SEXUAL CHILD ABUSE

Sexual child abuse is one type of abuse of people that occurs in our society. The small child is rarely away from the supervision of others for very long. Parents, siblings, neighbors, playground and day care supervisors are familiar with the children around them and observe their activities with a great deal of regularity. In cases of abuse of the elderly, those around them are mostly untrained and non-professionals in the detection of any kind of physical and sexual harassment, while persons around children are apt to be quickly aware with any change in attitude, appearance, or general mood. These are symptoms of problems that are affecting the child whether he reveals them or not. If a situation is disturbing, frightening, or even confusing to a child, those familiar with him or her should spot any changes quickly.

Katie

Mr. Kelly was surprised to get a call from Mr. Adams, the father of one of his kindergarten children, who requested a conference as soon as possible. At the meeting, Mr. Adams said, "I wanted this meeting to inform you that my wife and I are getting a divorce and think you should be aware of it for the welfare of our child." Mr. Kelly said that while school hadn't been in session too many weeks, Katie seemed to be making a good adjustment to it. However any change in her home environment could have an effect so he was glad to have any information that might assist him in working with her. He would be able to provide support and understanding on a sounder basis than would otherwise be true.

Mr. Adams then became even more serious and said, "I have to divorce my wife even though I love her very much, because of physical dangers to our children. Normally she is a mild and gentle person but occasionally she experiences violent outbursts of temper and actually throws the children around the room. Recently she threw our two year old boy against the wall on the other side of the living room. The situation is not being resolved, in fact, it seems to be getting worse and she will not seek professional help. The tragic consequence is that a divorce seems to be the only answer at this time."

This is an example of physical child abuse without any apparent sexual overtones. It suggests the problems people have in attempting to solve conflicts in their lives. But it also raises a question of whether a parent would come to the teacher to explain a case of sexual abuse of a child by the other parent. In this case, the teacher will be able to work with the child when signs of concern begin to appear. Knowing the cause will be very helpful for maintaining a good relationship and helping Katie grow up without as many traumatic consequences as would otherwise be the case. If the teacher becomes suspicious of problems at home because a child is bruised or extremely nervous or does not want to go home at the end of the day, but no clues exist as to the actual cause, there are real limitations to helping the child. A request for a conference may or may not reveal the problems, but if there is sexual abuse, it almost certainly will not become apparent.

Television, newspapers, magazines, and books have presented a substantial amount of material on child abuse in recent years, some quite factual and some emotion laden because it is an emotional subject. Certainly public awareness is higher than ever before, especially with regard to sexual child abuse. It is probably one of the most under-reported crimes in our society today. The general public finds it very hard to believe that people would commit sex crimes against infants and small children and view reports of incest or sodomy with a combination of disbelief and shock. Many parents and relatives do not wish sexual incidents against their children reported because (a) it may traumatize the child and lead to ostracization and embarrassment, and (b) it may stigmatize the family as a whole.

Figure 5-1 Photo courtesy of Committee for Children

It is believed that sexual child abuse is increasing, both in the number of cases and in the awareness of such cases (Finkelhor, 1984). Part of the increase is attributed to a more permissive society and part of it to less direct parental supervision. The greatest publicity is usually given to incest and parental exploitation by involving the child in child pornography, but child molesting by parents, relatives, neighbors, and others who have an opportunity is considered widespread. Senator Dodd, of Connecticut told a special session of Congress in 1984 that one case of child abuse out of five involves a child under the age of seven. Estimates as to the number of children that were sexually abused in 1988 ranged from a low of 45,000 to a high of 1,000,000.

In 1986 the American Humane Association conducted a study, funded by the National Center on Child Abuse and Neglect, of 132 thousand confirmed cases of child abuse. The age of the victims ranged from infancy through seventeen. Children seven or younger constituted 32.79 percent of the cases, or about one-third. The average age of the perpetrators was 32.5 with an age range from six to 98 years. Forty-two percent of the abusers were parents, including biological, foster, and adoptive. Over eighty percent of the perpetrators were male and over seventy-seven percent of the victims were female. In almost all cases, the younger children knew the abusers who had access to them in their home, neighborhood, or school.

The fondling of a child's genitals is the most common form of sexual child abuse and is sometimes initiated when the child is an infant. Such behavior is often disguised by the adults or juveniles involved as game-playing. Some form of oral sex is also a frequent sexual activity in which children are enticed or coerced to participate. In fact there seem to be no types of sexual abuse or sex crimes in which children have not been involved.

The reactions of children to sexual child abuse are quite varied. They may suffer from depression, anxiety, withdrawal; there may be a high degree of indifference; or there may be a positive reaction from pleasing the parents or whomever is pursuing the relationship. The reactions depend on several factors: the amount of physical trauma present, the relationship between the child and the abuser, the age of the child, the frequency of the activity, and the way the child is treated if the offense becomes public knowledge. The child may well be harmed more severely by the way people act toward him or her and the situation than the behavior itself. In addition, the personality of the child will strongly influence the nature and severity of the consequences. One of the complications in helping the child is the difficulty many people have in dealing with incest and other sexual abuses.

Gold (1986, p. 131) writes that, in addition to not talking with the sexually abused child, "a further complication is that we tend to treat children who are known to have been sexually abused in a different way. We are so afraid to add to the trauma that we overprotect them. We tend to blame all their misbehaviors on the sexual assault and are afraid to give them some limits they so desperately need. If the limits are not set, the child will continue to test the adults. An adult who does not enforce limits will not seem strong enough to those children, who are now searching for someone to protect them from further harm." In a letter to the authors, Gold pointed out that children often do not allow themselves to get over the trauma of sexual child abuse because they feel guilty for some other activity or thought that occurred prior to the abuse incident. This guilt may be associated with things as elementary as taking a piece of candy without permission or not coming straight home from school. The American culture stresses punishment for misdeeds, so children can intertwine misdeeds and punishment quite easily. Unless the therapist can identify the hidden activity for which the child has assumed the guilt for the sexual abuse, progress in alleviating the feelings of wrong-doing will be slow.

If a young child is involved in sexual abuses, any awareness of the nature and disapproval of such activities is very restricted. One may be willing to talk about it easily whereas older children are likely to be uncomfortable and even secretive. However the young child may begin to exhibit some degree of regression to behaviors that had been outgrown. The child may engage in some "baby talk," experience bed-wetting, or undergo a series of frightening nightmares. It is not unusual for the child to become more difficult to live with because of temper tantrums, loud-talking, the use of foul language, or becoming quite hyper-active in general.

Another possible consequence is that the child will begin to indulge in types of sex play that they normally would not at their age. They may display seductive types of behavior toward playmates, or even adults, or they may begin masturbating frequently and sometimes quite openly. These types of behaviors are often stimulated by the television programs and movies they have seen. In other words, even the small child becomes more sexually aware after being abused. Those working with a sexually abused child have a very fine line to walk in order to re-establish a growth toward a healthy sexuality for the age of the child. The child must recognize that what has happened is in the past, that there is not a stigmatization nor has he or she become abnormal; but rather, that life goes on and it is necessary to concentrate on learning about things to come. Boat and Everson (1988), in an article about interviewing abused children under six years of age, stress that they need much reassurance, and that promises that can't be kept should not be made, e.g., "no one will ever hurt you again." Most young children are able to adjust and the traumas of the abuses will disappear in a fairly short period of time.

In a broader perspective, it is clear that sexual abuse has no social, economic, or racial parameters. Until recently, it was believed that sexual abuse of children would most likely come from strangers, including the proverbial, "dirty old man." The most common prevention was essentially verbal: "Don't talk to strangers," "Don't take candy from anyone you don't know," or "Don't get into any car without our permission." However, as we learn more about the sexual abuse of children, it becomes more and more apparent that the most common abusers are those who are close to the child such as family members, relatives, and neighbors. Most of those who have been identified in court and through research have been young and consistently under the age of fifty. One study found that only ten per cent of those involved were over the age of fifty. It is possible to educate the young child with regard to preventing sexual abuse but it is very difficult to identify the persons from whom the attacks may come.

PEDOPHILES

A pedophile is defined as a person who engages in the seduction and sexual abuse of children. It is a form of addiction in which the preferred sexual object is a child. A pedophile is most commonly an adult male who is attracted to female children - or less often - to a male child, but rarely to both. A pedophile's range of behavior includes looking at photographs and videos of children engaged in sexual activities, or pouring over books which contain such pictures with a text. There is a substantial amount of material available for this purpose; the most explicit being obtainable only by mail or in some adult stores. These materials are used for self stimulation by the pedophiles but also are used to show to children as a means of reassuring the young people that these are common and acceptable behaviors.

One type of pedophile is the "child molester" who is usually a fixated person who was himself abused as a child and who continues to engage in the behavior over a period of many years. Often they are "loners" even though they may be, or have been, married and sometimes have become parents. They have become fixated on prepubescent young people and may become involved with a child for many months before any sexual advances and physical behaviors occur.

Another type of pedophile is the "regressed molester" who may have no overt sexual involvement with children until some severe stress or major crisis occurs in his life. A failure to cope with the problem leads to his sexual orientation toward children becoming manifest. He will behave as a molester for a period of time but may cease overt activities after the stressful period has passed.

Gary

Mr. James was an elementary school teacher who had been in the same school system for twenty-five years. Suddenly he began taking young boys, one at a time, into an unused room during the lunch hour. He told the kindergarten teacher in the next room that he was tutoring the children. Although Mr. James was liked and respected, when this activity continued, the principal was informed and he told the teacher to cease immediately. Shortly after a little boy, Gary, told his parents that Mr. James had taken him into an empty room, closed the door, and began to hug and kiss him on the mouth, while telling the child how much he loved him. The boy became frightened, ran out of the room, and later told his parents. The parents informed the principal and the school administration, but insisted they did not wish to pursue the matter further. Mr. James was placed on sick leave and required to seek counselling if he ever wished to return to the teaching profession.

Certainly there are many people who have pedophilic feelings but manage to suppress them for their entire life. Others such as Mr. James become active in seeking young children after many years of inactivity for reasons that are not clear. One of the strong deterrents to pedophilic behavior is the fear of the consequences if discovered. This is a type of behavior that is denounced by employers, colleagues, neighbors, and even family; so that a revealed pedophile will be subject to widespread condemnation. A pedophile in prison is widely shunned by the other prisoners and may actually be harmed by them.

Researchers now believe they are compiling an accurate profile of the child molester (Finkelhor, 1979). He is likely to be fairly young, hold a legitimate position in the community but one which provides an opportunity to pursue his sexual orientation. In a majority of cases, a sexual molester is known to the child and most are around the child on a frequent or even daily basis. They are also often repeat offenders who were abused as a child. One study tallied seventy-three victims for each heterosexual molester and thirty for each homosexual one. Although males are by far the most prevalent child molesters, there is evidence that females are becoming increasingly involved with children. In both sexes, there is a psychological profile of a weak, insecure person, fearful that he or she is unloved but who needs to be in control of a situation. Involvement with small children fulfills these needs very effectively.

ABOUT INCESTUOUS RELATIONSHIPS

Incest, the sexual relations between persons related by blood in some degree as defined by law, has been known throughout history but almost always as an unacceptable activity. It is not an unknown type of behavior in any part of the world, nor is it limited to any class, race, religion, or cultural grouping. Most often those involved in an incestuous relationship are brother and sister, or parent and child. Less frequently involved, at least statistically, are aunts, uncles, and grandparents. Stepfathers are sometimes found to be sexually associated with their stepchildren and this is treated as incest even though there is not a direct blood relationship. Sexual relations between blood relations who are forbidden to marry is the minimal consideration for incest but usually is extended to a greater degree. (See Figure 5-2)

Vaginal intercourse is the primary focus in an incestuous relation in a family, but oral and anal sex have also been recorded in parental and kinship associations. There is a case on record of a mother having oral sex with her four month old son. Reports of this kind of behavior are assumed to be quite rare by most people but recent studies suggest that frequency of incest and the forms it takes would not have been believed a few years ago. As with most forms of sexual behavior involving children, reporting of it to the public is quite sporadic, often unreliable, and limited to the extreme or bizarre incidents. The adults who participate go to great lengths to conceal their activities and children are discouraged from revealing the incestuous behavior in a variety of ways. Adults may use threats of physical punishment, or bribery with money or presents to discourage the children from exposing the relationship, but frequently the young child is unaware of the seriousness of the situation, especially if it is a parent who is involved. Often there is a love or affection among the participants and neither wishes to do anything that may cause harm or bring shame to the other (or themselves).

Young children who have become involved in incestuous situations will be less aware of the significance or illegality of such behavior than older children. On the other hand, they are unlikely to be sufficiently sophisticated or secretive that they can keep it to themselves. In fact, they are quite likely to provide clues to others that unusual things have occurred. Persons who work with a small child or know them well will quickly become aware that something different is happening in the child's life. It is not hard to persuade the young child to admit and describe the details of an incestuous relationship through careful questioning, plus careful listening to the answers.

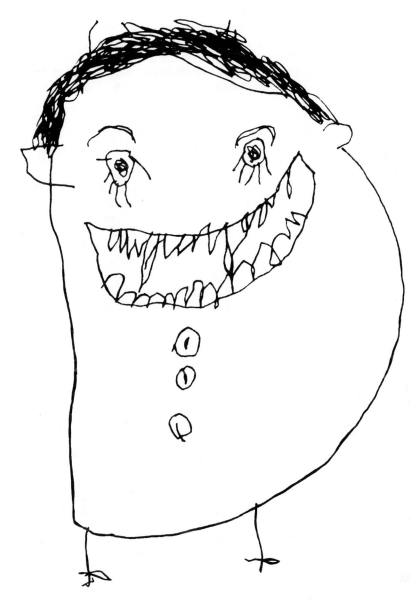

This four year old girl's favorite pastime was drawing pictures and she often drew people with large heads and mouths. Authorities informed her day care teacher that the child had been sexually abused. The child's father forced and bribed her to perform oral sex on him. This began when the child was three and ended when the father was removed from the home when the child was four years of age.

Figure 5-2 Oral sex with father

The committing of incest with a child six years of age or under is less common than with an older child. This is the age, however, where incestuous intentions may easily begin with games or teasing or physical expressions of affection with sexual overtones. Later any or all of these may develop into an incestuous relationship. When the specific motivation in physical expressions of love and affection is sexual arousal and gratification, and this develops over a period of time during such contacts, it is defined as incestual motivation. This kind of motivation is not present in a normal physical relationship between parent and child, even though there is frequently touching, kissing, and other such physical contacts which are intended to express love and affection. Without the motivation of incest, this type of relationship is an integral part of the development of a healthy sexuality in a child. It is important to recognize that the adult or older person controls the nature of an association with a young child and must be held responsible for any deviations beyond acceptable limits.

Marta

The story told to her teacher by four year old Marta was an example of an expression of love and affection which was beyond those limits. As she often did, Marta came over to her teacher on the playground to talk. This time she started by saying, "Mrs. Beck, I want to tell you something but my Daddy told me not tell anyone." The teacher responded quickly that if her Daddy told her not to tell then she shouldn't tell her. Marta said, "He isn't my real Daddy. He and my sister like each other very much and they go into the bedroom and lock the door and I can't come in. I wish they would let me in the bedroom too because I love my Daddy very much too. He hugs and kisses me a lot and tells me he loves me a lot."

The teacher decided not to pursue the conversation. She was very concerned but the child was very hesitant and uncertain about the situation she had referred to with her stepfather. Other children came along at that point and brought up other things so the conversation ended.

The next day on the playground, Marta again came over to Mrs. Beck when no other children were present and said, "I want to tell you the secret Daddy and I have. It is a secret game - I touch Daddy's big 'pee-wee' and he touches me down there. It feels good but I feel funny when I touch Daddy. I want to tell you because you are my teacher but don't tell anyone else our secret."

The teacher knew that if the little girl was being molested, it was her duty to report it. She decided to confer with the school counsellor and conveyed the details of Marta's conversation with her. The counsellor said she would work with the child and arranged a preliminary session for the next day. When Marta was comfortable and relaxed, the counsellor introduced some anatomically correct dolls and began a discussion about families in general and Marta's in particular. (See Figure 5-3) Ultimately the little girl related her secret relationship with her stepfather and what was included in it. The counsellor pursued such matters as frequency of occurrence, the length of time it had been going on, and whether it was a current situation. Marta said she had played the secret yesterday while her mother was working and her older sister was at school. The counsellor then went on to other matters and introduced some other toys and topics of discussion. (See Figure 5-4)

It is mandatory for school personnel to report suspected cases of child abuse in this school system so the counsellor contacted the HRS (Health and Rehabilitation Service) who began an investigation. The children were removed from the home during this time so there could be no abusive activity continued. In this case the older girl, age nine, told the investigators that she had been involved with her stepfather for over a year. She said, "Daddy put his penis between my legs and gave me money if I wouldn't tell anyone and I didn't." The stepfather was sent to prison and the mother and two girls underwent intensive counselling.

The reasons a member of a family begins an incestuous relationship with a child are very difficult to ascertain in individual cases. It is very hard to obtain adequate data on which to base a theory; it is very hard to know if a sample is representative of the population who may be involved. Some men's magazines sometimes print letters from readers touching upon incest but they are almost always from the victims, not the perpetrators. Some women report incestuous relations with their father and attempt to tie it to a present situation or problem. Others report a very satisfactory involvement with the father which was not terminated until the daughter began dating or left home. Letters such as these seldom reveal any significant information about the nature and causes of incest other than to suggest that the frequency is higher then that officially reported to authorities. A beginning Social Worker will rarely be on the job for more than a month without encountering a case of incest in some form.

Figure 5-3 Anatomically correct dolls (Photo courtesy of June Hornest, Teach A Bodies Co.)

A six year old girl reported to her Aunt that the picture was of herself and the baby she would have when she married daddy. She said, "We love each other and we play our secret game because it feels good." This was a "street-wise" child who assumed much of her working mother's role at home. The mother and step-father are now separated because of the incestuous behavior that occurred.

Figure 5-4 Girl with baby's head

When incest does occur in the home, it is common, especially in the case of young children, for threats to be made to the child to prevent any public revelation. Older children may well be able to foresee the consequences of a court trial or newspaper headline, and the possible imprisonment of a family member. The mother is often unaware of what is going on, especially the working mother whose absence is the time the incestuous behaviors take place. However there are cases in which the mother is fully aware of what is taking place and does nothing about it, either because of fear of harm to herself, or a high degree of indifference to the child. Sexual behavior to a young child is devoid of the implications it has for older people, but it may have a degree of pleasure, a special secret, or perhaps some type of guilt feelings. The last situation will often occur if a little child has been told not to tell and then reveals the behavior. It is essential to take into account the child's welfare when an incident of incest is made public. The child will need professional counselling to help understand the recent events and to prepare for the future. Perhaps the most vital need for the child is to develop a sound sexual identity, to be able to put sex into a socially acceptable context, and to relate to other people without secrecy, shame, or a sense of wrongdoing. The thing that makes this so extraordinarily difficult is the fact that the "condemned" behavior was with a family member, a person who is integral in the establishment of a loving relationship. (See Figure 5-5)

In her research into incest and child molestation, Masters (1986) found that most perpetrators were products of emotionally, physically and/or sexually abusive environments, that they lacked communicative skills, had poor esteem, and were generally unable to achieve intimate relationships with other people. It was also noted that a number had sexual problems, and many were alcohol and drug abusers. Contrary to common belief, a substantial number of men turn to their children for sexual purposes rather than resort to masturbation, prostitution, or extra-marital sexual affairs because these are considered contrary to their religious beliefs or moral standards.

In a recent book, Finkelhor (1984) cites repressive home environments as the major cause of sexual abuse of children. Many of the abusers are members of the family. Where home environments are sexually restricted and repressive and emphasize traditional sex roles, sexual child abuse may occur within the family, and the children are not resistant because they are taught to obey and comply. Two other factors mentioned by Finkelhor are a possibly greater vulnerability for a little girl if there is a stepfather present, and if there is a pronounced educational inferiority on the part of the wife. Gordon (1989) reported that in cases where the natural father abused a child, he was more likely to be under greater stress than an abusing stepfather, e.g., drug-user, alcoholic, mental problems, and low income.

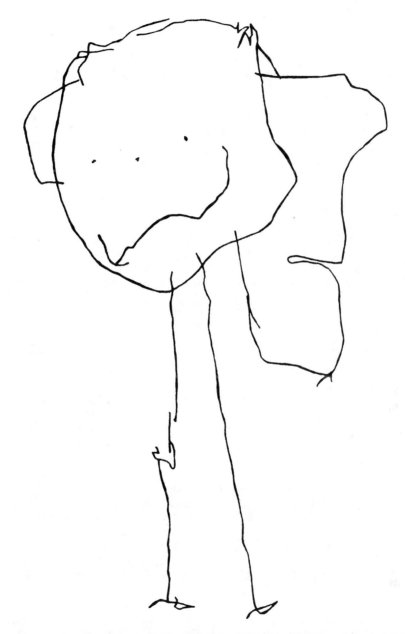

This five year old boy told his teacher that he had made a picture of himself. The child had been sexually abused by his fifteen year old brother.

Figure 5-5 Boy with large head

Some experts in family law who have evaluated reports of sexual child abuse say that fathers involved in divorce cases are sometimes wrongly accused of child molestation by the wife as a legal tactic. False allegations are also made in child custody cases to avoid any kind of sharing or visitation rights. It has been estimated that the number of false charges had increased from ten to thirty per cent in recent years. It is suspected that most such charges are false but fathers are quite vulnerable to them because of the general association of child care and protection with the mother. Extreme hostility between the parents makes the truth hard to ascertain.

CHILD PORNOGRAPHY

Occasionally young children need protection from family members who exhibit incestuous tendencies as well as from other adults who involve their own children and others in child pornographic activities. The last few years have seen a substantial increase in public awareness of this area of child abuse inasmuch as pictures of participants and victims and a parade of charges and countercharges plus numerous denials have appeared in the media with increasing frequency. In some of the incidents, the children involved have been six years of age and even younger in a few cases. It has been fully documented that some parents do engage in sexual acts with their own children and often photograph their behaviors; trading these photographs with other adults or selling them to magazines that publish them on a regular basis. Such child pornography is currently illegal in many states and most others are considering action or taking steps to curtail these activities. In addition, it is against the postal laws to distribute such photographs through the mails.

In 1978, when the law for Protection of Children Against Sexual Exploitation was passed, it was hoped that this type of child abuse would be eliminated. Although a number of commercial dealers in child pornographic pictures and magazines did drop out of sight, many hard-core pedophiles became more active and more than picked up the slack. The Child Protection Act of 1984 provided for federal involvement by making the transportation of child pornographic literature and other materials through the mails illegal. This is a hard law to police because such materials are traditionally sent in a "plain brown wrapper" and therefore undetectable on the surface. The most common exposure occurs when they are received by the wrong person who then files a complaint with the postal authorities.

Many pedophiles collect and exchange these materials so the relationship between child pornography and child abuse is quite substantial. With the films of sexual activities, the pedophile can review and relive his activities and those of others with children on a repeated basis. Films can be obtained from specialized stores which advertise such pictures as "The Cradle Snatchers" and "Never Too Young." There is also a substantial number of books with similar titles and also containing pornographic pictures. An organization in California which claims 5000 members has as its slogan, "Sex by Eight or Its Too Late." Spokesmen for the group claim that children are receptive to sex by age one or two and that such relationships are both normal and desirable. Organizations such as this are essentially a front for pedophiles, and while their membership claims are exaggerated, they do exist and indulge in sexual child abuse.

A study by the American Psychiatric Association in 1984 concluded that over fifty per cent of the children in their sample of sixty-six who were involved with a sex ring of adults, were also employed in the making of pornographic films. There is no substantial evidence that it is harmful for a young child to see a pornographic film but there is always the danger that the showing of the film is a device to convince the child that it is all right to become involved himself. The pedophile will contend that the children in the picture wouldn't have done it if it wasn't acceptable or even that it is "great fun." If a child is photographed during his participation in sex acts with children and/or adults, the consequences in the future may be quite severe. Sometimes the pedophile will show the films to the child over a period of time with the threat to expose him to others if he ever tells anyone. Further, the child will ultimately begin to wonder who else has seen the pictures and if he or she was recognized and what might happen in the years to come. Perhaps the most difficult situations are those in which one or both parents are involved and the child comes to realize the illegality of the behaviors and the probability of punishment for the parents as well as the destruction of his or her own reputation. It is not unusual for the child to blame himself or herself and develop severe guilt feelings when sexual child abuse is made public, especially if the child had warned not to reveal anything about the activities that had taken place. A young child takes seriously a promise to keep a secret or "it's just between us" because it is such an important part of being accepted as part of a group. (See Figure 5-6)

The total number of pedophiles in a geographic area cannot be determined with any real degree of accuracy. A Senate Committee once estimated that there were fewer than 2000 nationwide. On the other hand, the Justice Department obtained 147 convictions against child pornographers in the two years following the passage of the Child Protection Act of 1984.

Finally it should be stressed that the ramifications of pedophilic activities and pornographic materials extend far beyond the

This five year old girl told her baby sitter this was a picture of her grandfather. She added, "Grandpa, another man and I took off our clothes and played games and took pictures." The baby sitter repeated the conversation and gave the pictures to the child's mother.

Figure 5-6 Man with penis

psychological damage that may be done to the child and the criminal charges that may disrupt families and friends. Incidents of sexual child abuse are often accompanied by the spread of venereal disease, by physical injuries including rectal tears and lacerated vaginas, and currently may facilitate the spread of AIDS among the children. When these tragic conditions are added to the phobias, nightmares, and neuroses that may accompany such abuses, the cost is quite great. One additional cost occurs if the parents are involved and the child lived at home, namely, there will likely be a need for child placement in a foster home which is quite difficult to achieve and not always satisfactory.

THE PREVENTION OF CHILD ABUSE

There are many programs in current use in both public and private schools which are designed to educate kindergarten and elementary children and their parents on ways to prevent sexual abuse and how to cope with it if it should occur. These are not intended to be sex education programs, but preventive measures. A young child can develop a useful though limited vocabulary of proper terms for the male and female sex organs and other relevant parts of the body. These terms and some knowledge of sexual behaviors will enable them to communicate with others in a positive manner. One of the purposes and expected values of such programs is that it may encourage the child to initiate questions which lead to a discussion of sexuality and sexual behavior which the child has stimulated and enters into as a participant.

For these programs to be successful and their goals achieved, the parents must be involved and encouraged to allow their children to participate. Children should always be required to have their parents written permission for such programs. The programs should be widely publicized through Parent-Teacher organizations, school communications, and as handouts for the children to take home. Those directing the activities must be qualified and at ease with young children to achieve maximum benefits.

One plan that has been used in pre-school and school systems is "Happy Bear: Teaching Pre-School Children About Sexual Areas" by Helen L. Swan (1984). The primary objective in this program is to teach young children the three "R's" of prevention - recognition, resisting, and reporting. If the young child is not taught the essential details of sexual abuse, the chances of becoming a victim are substantially increased. The basic weakness of young persons and their vulnerability is an innocence and lack of awareness of the total range of human behavior and its consequences. They do not know the danger signals, or the means of prevention, and can be tempted by promises of candy, games, and especially the idea that it is fun or approved behavior for everyone.

Figure 5-7 (Courtesy of Helen L. Swan, Kansas Child Abuse Prevention Council)

Kindergarten age children or younger are normally very uncomfortable in reporting sexual assaults or abusive behavior because they have little grasp of the nature and significance of such behavior. Through the use of such techniques as hand puppets, anatomically correct dolls, role-playing, and other sophisticated procedures for bringing out the details of a child's experiences and some of the implications, a small child can be brought to some level of realization of what has happened and what it means. On the other hand, it is very, very important that the child not be traumatized about sexual behavior and relationships among people. Learning experiences, even those devoted to problems of sexual abuse, must be directed toward the positive aspects of growth and sexual adjustments in the future.

A technique known as "touching" has been employed quite successfully in helping young children learn the distinction between "good" and "bad" physical contacts among people. Basically this refers to situations which make you feel comfortable, secure, and unthreatened, in contrast to those which result in angry, anxious, or sad feelings, or result in pain or actual physical injury. A related aspect of touching is known as "confused touching" and includes situations in which the child is made uncomfortable or is unsure what the situation means. An example might be a kiss which lasts for a long time, or a tickling which becomes uncomfortable.

An excellent program in this area is found in Talking About Touching - A Personal Safety Curriculum (1988) and is appropriate for working with an individual child or a group of children ages preschool - kindergarten. The object of the program is to help young children, and older children too, to learn about "child molesters, private body parts, and to distinguish private from public body parts." The complete set includes plastic-coated pictures and a manual which depict children and adults in a variety of situations. The pictures are shown to the child and a guided discussion of the subject of the picture is carried on by the child and the adults working in the program. On the back of each picture is a carefully developed lesson plan. The goal is given, along with definitions, the appropriate age group, and notes for the teacher. A program such as this must be carefully followed so the young child is not encouraged to pursue matters beyond an appropriate level of comprehension. In other words, it is necessary to protect against the development of unreasonable fears, or the reading of dangers into normal and acceptable situations, and also to avoid an overstressing of the importance of a situation. When this program has been used properly, the children have been quite receptive and acquired the intended goals and concepts easily.

There are several dangers in the educating of a young child about sexual child abuse and they are usually quite subtle in nature. Children must be warned about sexual abuse and yet not become frightened of sex and sex relations. They must learn about private body parts and "bad" touching but not become ashamed of the human body nor be afraid of physical contacts which express love, warmth, and security. How to avoid dangers of scaring a child are not easy to determine, but we do know that a child needs guidance in the early years in both the home environment and in the school. If the approaches to sexual abuse and its prevention are done in a tension free manner, and the personality of the child is taken into account, it is possible for the child to understand and appreciate what is being taught without over-reacting.

It is important for both parents and professionals who work with young children to know that the professionals are required to report instances of child abuse to the proper authorities in all fifty states. In most states, a failure to report such abuses is a misdemeanor, punishable by a jail term of six months to a year plus a monetary fine. Loss of job is also a possibility. However if professionals make reports in good faith, they are protected from any future legal consequences. Ordinarily, a public school system will have its policies spelled out in the Teacher's Manual and will include guidelines for reporting actual and suspected cases of child abuse. These guidelines are extremely important because you are dealing with young children who have vivid imaginations at times, and who are easily influenced by others to say what they think persons want to hear, not necessarily describe what really happened. If the teacher is confronted with physical evidence or supporting testimony, the reporting is simplified. In addition to reporting cases of child abuse for the well-being of the child and future protection, it also enables the authorities to provide counselling and take any steps recommended by mental health professionals. The practices and policies of private schools are difficult to categorize inasmuch as they range from exclusive upper class academies to small rural religious schools in a conservative community, so there are fewer common standards.

PREVENTIVE SUGGESTIONS FOR PARENTS AND TEACHERS

The suggestions offered below are intended to help parents and teachers prevent sexual child abuse of young children and also to enable prompt detection of instances in which it does occur.

1.   Know where the child is and the person(s) he or she is with.

2. Use correct terminology whenever discussing or describing any aspects of sex organs or sex behavior. This can be extended to any references to any part of the body and even human relations in general, as a means of reducing distortions and prejudices.

3. Instruct children very specifically as to who has the right to touch or examine their body, especially the genital and rectal areas. Persons such as nurses and physicians, baby sitters, family and relatives can be associated with situations of touching, such as bathing, attending to a medical problem, or other emergency, and changing clothes. Some people have recommended as a guideline, "those parts of the body that are covered by the bathing suit" are private and personal.

4. Teach the child that one should be equally respectful of the same parts of the body of other people and should not become involved in examining or touching them. The stress should be on privacy and personal rights rather than the dangers or evil aspects.

5. Explain how and when to say no if situations of touching sexual areas arise, and also how to leave the area and persons involved at once. The child should also be advised to report all such incidents to the parents or teachers.

6. If a child uses sexually explicit language, slang, vulgarity, and four-letter words which are not used in the home, seek to uncover the source of such language.

7. Arrange an appointment with a physician if a child is sore or bruised in the genital or rectal areas or if there are infections or discharges.

8. Listen carefully when a child speaks about situations or persons that are unfamiliar or unusual, and be especially alert to any references that may have sexual overtones.

9. Pay attention to any unusual fears or anxieties and seek out the causes and cures. Seek an explanation without creating stress or concern on the part of the child.

10. Seek reasons for excesses or increases in masturbation.

11. Remember that a child who has been abused, sexually or otherwise, needs love, care, and understanding, not accusations or threats.

12. It is most important for parents and other adults concerned to retain their self-control if their child is molested or abused.

13. In the same vein, make sure that siblings and other children do not socially or psychologically abuse the child who has been sexually abused. The teacher's role in the classroom and on the playground is critical.

14. Seek professional help in coping with any signs of disturbance in an abused child. Understand that both early and late reactions can take many directions so any change in behavior, attitudes, or relationships may be a clue that help is needed.

15. Avail yourself of Child-Abuse Hotlines and special Counseling Centers that may be available in your area. Parents Anonymous (P.A.) has a toll-free number (1-800-421-0353) and there are also some local chapters around the country.

16. Mental Health Centers and Associations are a good source of referrals and guidance. The address and phone number can be found in the telephone directory, usually in both the White and Yellow Pages. In some cases, the emergency number (911) may be appropriate.

17. To help parents, there is a national Child Abuse Registry which can be contacted by phone (1-800-342-9152).

QUESTIONS FOR DISCUSSION

1. If a teacher suspects sexual child abuse of one or more of the young children with whom he or she works, what are the responsibilities and what are the limitations in dealing with it?

2. If a young child reports an instance of a man exposing himself to one or more of the students, what are the teachers' options in relation to the child, the entire class, the parents, and the administration? List and evaluate them.

3. Although a young child has limited awareness, what are some of the possible affects of the following: (a) incest, (b) pornography, and (c) sexual abuse.

4. In the general approach to sexual abuse of children, what are the strengths and weaknesses of Talking About Touching, anatomically correct dolls, and parent-teacher conferences?

5. List the causes of incest and describe preventive approaches.

6. How might young children contribute to or even cause the kinds of situation discussed in this chapter?

CHAPTER REFERENCES

Boat, B. & M.D. Everson (1988). Interviewing young children with anatomical dolls. Child Welfare, 67: 337-352.

Finkelhor, D. (1979). Sexually victimized children. New York: Free Press.

Finkelhor, D. (1984). Child sexual abuse: new theory and research. New York: Free Press.

Finkelhor, D. (1984). How widespread is child sexual abuse? Children Today, 13: 18-20.

Gold, S. (1986). When children invite abuse: a search for answers when love is not enough. Eugene, OR: Fern Ridge Press.

Gordon, M. (1989). The family environment of sexual abuse: a comparison of natural and stepfather abuse. Child Abuse and Neglect, 13: 121-130.

Masters, J.V. (1986). Forum feedback. Playboy, 33: November. 42-46.

Staff, Committee for Children (1988). Talking about touching: a personal safety curriculum. Seattle, WA.

Swan, L.H. (1984). Happy Bear: teaching pre-school children about sexual abuse. Topeka, KS: Kansas Child Abuse Prevention Council.

CHAPTER VI

THE CURRENT SCENE AND YOUNG CHILDREN

The primary intention of the authors in developing the final two chapters is to provide up-to-date information on current issues that have an impact on young children, both directly and indirectly. The issues discussed influence the child's sexuality as it develops, although various children will be affected in different ways. The information presented in Chapters Six and Seven offer few conclusions, but are attempts to present the various considerations in the problems that exist in today's world. The information was acquired from many sources and modified and adapted to apply to our subject, the young child. The material was continually updated until the last minute as the issues are current, controversial, and dynamic. Sources include radio and television programs and specials, library research in professional books and journals from several disciplines, daily newspapers, weekly news magazines, and from interviews, correspondence, and telephone conversations with experts in the various areas. The authors believe that all the topics discussed are important for the future of young children and the way they are resolved will be significant for their sexuality.

Throughout human history, attitudes toward and treatment of young children have varied from era to era and from society to society (Leslie, 1979). However, in most historical periods, there has been one or two preferred patterns in each social grouping. Young people have been loved and spoiled at one time, ignored at another, and mistreated or abused during yet another. A particular trend may last for centuries or only a few decades. There have been civilizations which approved and practiced

132

Figure 6-1 *(Photo courtesy of Virginia Lively)*

abortion and infanticide (the killing of babies shortly after birth). In many societies of the past, male children were preferred, so girl babies were often killed or abandoned, especially if there were already one or two female children in the family. Attitudes toward children have also varied in relation to social and economic conditions. Children were unwanted during depressions because they were an extra mouth to feed, but wanted after a war to help replenish the population losses due to combat casualties. Children have been sold into slavery, apprenticed out as workers, and sometimes just kicked out the door and told to not come back.

In Colonial America, children were wanted to help populate the new country, but they were not treated as equals in any sense. Little children were required to eat at a sideboard or in the kitchen, sleep in unheated lofts, and speak only when spoken to. With the exception of wealthy families, survival was very difficult and babies and youngsters shared in all the hardships. Very young children helped with the chores, tended newborn babies, and went to church for many hours at a time. School was limited or non-existent, so all the children were thrown together each day in and around the home. Many children were born but the extremely high death rate kept most families within limits of their income and maintenance.

The Industrial Revolution brought cities and urban crowding. Children were an economic liability until they were able to work in a factory. This could occur as early as five years of age. On the other hand, the movement Westward into new territories required more and more people to farm and provide services, so children became quite useful, especially as they became older and more capable. All in all, the status of children in the United States was not too different at the turn of the 20th century than it had been throughout history, but the seeds for dramatic changes had been sown.

THE YOUNG CHILD'S WORLD IN THE LATE 1980s

In the Twentieth Century, a Mechanical Revolution has taken place, a Technological Revolution has occurred, an Electronic and Computer Revolution has started, and all are continuing. A major consequence has been a need for more education with the necessary scientific and technical skills. School systems are expanding, compulsory education is emphasized, and teachers are becoming more specialized. Children gradually became the responsibility of their parents well into their teens - contributing to a desire for smaller families. Most importantly, an ever-increasing number of women began to work outside the home, including mothers with young children. The care and feeding of these children was shared among in-home child care providers, child care centers, and pre-school programs, in addition to siblings, relatives, and neighbors. Technological advances and better health care resulted in more children surviving and also allowed births to be planned, spaced as desired, and limited to a preferred number. The term "Generation Gap" has been used and abused for quite a number of years, but it probably has more applicability than ever before. To use one simple illustration, elementary school boys and girls are studying computer usage and the associated languages, but many of their parents are uncomfortable with computers and the grandparents are generally out of their depth.

Recognizing the impossibility of covering all the important developments of the Twentieth Century, the remainder of this section will be devoted to three major influences of the period with special emphasis on young children. These influences are identified as:

1. The emphasis on human rights that has occurred on a wide-spread basis and includes the welfare of children in social, political, and legal activities.

2. The ability to communicate many things in many ways to people in their own homes, thus necessitating substantial revisions in

the educational process to take advantage of children's greater awareness of many things (with or without comprehension).

3. The enveloping of people in general, and children in particular, with materialism, artificiality, and a powerful economic component in the value system of societies, thus creating more pressure on families than has ever existed before.

There has been a powerful striving for equality and human rights throughout the world and the United States has not escaped the pressures, rather, it has often been a leader. A reduction of biases and discriminatory behaviors toward women, minorities, cultural groups, and age groups has been pushed, not always successfully, but with continuing pressures. The idea that everyone is a person, and has a personality distinct from all others, has been extended in various ways to infants and young children. Young people have been increasingly protected in wills and the distribution of an inheritance. The whole area of Federal Aid to the children of the poor has been expanded over the years, although it has its detractors as well as defenders. Suits have been filed on behalf of children injured in accidents, and on behalf of children whose parents have been killed or injured in accidents. The rights of children are becoming accepted and are appearing in a new variety of ways each year. Parents have been sued because they did not provide their child with sufficient intelligence for him or her to be successful. Schools have been sued because they did not educate a child to his optimal potential. Automobile drivers have been sued after hitting a child who ran out from between two cars because they should have been aware of a little child's carelessness. Some such lawsuits are won and some are lost in the courts, but in each case the child is considered as a legal entity and his rights are fully considered.

A second major influence is the tremendous growth of forces that stimulate the young child's awareness. He has been exposed to life and death, different styles of living, crimes of all kinds and trials of criminals, cultural phenomenon from around the world, plus a wide range of personalities. The young child of today has seen old and new movies, live TV programs and reruns of the past, and even the children's shows that his parents grew up with are available. The increase in VCRs has brought totally uncensored films into the home. The commonness of the automobile has permitted travel across the U.S.A. and many children have been on airplanes and ships to foreign countries.

Another source of sophistication for the child is the variety of supervisors and teachers to whom he or she is exposed. The proliferation of child care centers and nurseries has been mentioned, but one of the most important aspects of these supervisory agencies is the specialized personnel that help rear the child. For music and art, physical activities, field trips, punishment and rewards, there will be different people in charge. When the numerous child care providers, tour guides, bus drivers, amusement park ride operators, and the like are combined with parents and teachers, the youngster is exposed to many persons of varied backgrounds and abilities. The little boys and girls see the good and the bad, the pretty and the ugly, the reasonable and the ridiculous, and they are not coordinated into a meaningful whole. In other words, the sexuality of the child is being developed at a more rapid pace than before, but without the constant supervision of the mother or the parents together, or even the neighborhood. The coordination of a teacher's activities and procedures with specialists, other teachers, and administrative policies has increased in complexity, but become more necessary.

The parents of the latter part of the 20th century have become aware of the impact of these many influences, but at the same time they have less time to spend with their children. This situation has brought emphasis on "quality time," or the idea of making maximum use of the time they do have. Some experts have contended that the crucial consideration for the parents is to find ways to express love and affection and to reassure children that they are wanted and loved. They are advised to be sure to take the time to listen to a recital of the day's events and to go places and do things with the child as often as possible. Unfortunately, this type of counselling has led to parental guilt feelings and created pressures that cannot be resolved easily with the time available. When Daddy says, " I am very interested in how you cut your finger and what happened on the playground, but right now I have to go to a meeting," the child may get the feeling that he really is not interested, especially if it happens frequently. The mother may not be a source of comfort, because she too has to go to a meeting or go to work, or catch up on family chores because she has been gone all day. The crux of the problem in most families is the failure to establish an environment for the child with a consistency that can be understood.

The third force that is especially prominent in recent years is the change in the physical and material world in which we live. Most young children today are reared in the midst of cement, brick, buildings, streets, and artificial materials. They learn what they know about nature from TV, zoos, and some observations if they travel through the country (many city children do not). The toys, clothes, dishes, furniture, and other surroundings in the home are made of materials created by man. The child is surrounded by plastics, nylons and orlons, laminated products, polyethelene goods, and food prepared with additives and preservatives of all kinds. The young child sees super-markets, flea markets, discount houses, automobile marts, drive-in banks, restaurants and the like. An awareness of life is very influenced by the apparent fact that anything is available at a price. Things that don't work are replaced or repaired at a cost. It is very difficult to do things for yourself, it has to be paid for with money, so a materialistic orientation is inevitable. There is a serious question as to whether the young child can separate the artificiality of his material world from the naturalness of people. Some people do try to replace the limitations and defects of nature with face lifts, hair coloring, girdles, and shoes with lifts, as well as the more pertinent use of eye glasses, bridges and false teeth, organ removal, or a substitution when deficient. With the exception of psychiatric and psychological counselling, the personality of people is the result of their sexuality as it developed over the years. Does the young person really grasp that "what you see is what you get" with regard to people? If Daddy doesn't earn enough money for a new bicycle, the child must learn you can't trade him in or buy a new one, but must accept him as he is, for better or worse. Teachers at all levels must be careful that they do not become overly dependent on mechanical, technical, electronic, and high-tech gadgets. These are useful, but it is humans that are being educated.

The continued striving for human rights, the greater awareness of the world and its diversity, and the increase in artificiality in the environment are truly significant in the development of a child in today's world. But they do not obscure the fact that in the family and in the home, there remains a comfortableness and a familiarity that is natural and will persist through time. The child in the slums and the child in the suburbs believes his or her parents love him or her and he or she loves them. The child who has been abused and the child who has been deprived believes this. This love and affection can be damaged or destroyed over time, but this is very hard to do. It is possible for families to plan their time together and to control their activities, but the real need is for communication. Does the child understand why he is being punished? Does he or she know what can be gained by staying with the child care provider or go to the child care center? Is it explained that there is more to life than fancy clothes and expensive toys? A little boy needs to know what it means to be a boy and how to relate to girls, other boys, adults, friends, strangers, and what will happen as he grows up. These needs are equally important for the female child. If those who work with the child when young can provide a logical or coherent base into which the child can put the new ideas and objects when exposed to them, then a sound sexuality is being built. New things should challenge or intrigue, rather than frighten. Every parent can build on the love and trust given by a young child and it is a major responsibility not to abuse it.

THE REDEFINING OF MASCULINE AND FEMININE ROLES

Changes in the traditional masculine and feminine ways of thinking and behaving have been a prominent part of the 1980s. The male, as the patriarchal head of the family, is becoming the exception rather than the rule. The wife as a passive homemaker and mother also occurs less frequently. Three sociologists report on a study that has some interesting implications for the future of family structure. They found that modern young people place more emphasis on personal freedom, rational choice, and hedonistic values than on children. Both husbands and wives rated children as more valuable than extra money, a neat house, and fulfilling hobbies by a small margin, and nearly half rated freedom of movement, use of leisure time, and employment opportunities for the wife as equal or more valuable than children (Neal, Groat & Wicks, 1989). The direction that these changes ultimately take is not easy to predict; thus, it is not clear whether the guidance provided to young children today will be that which they need for the adult world as it will be when they grow up.

The basic unpredictability derives from two trends that are not entirely compatible with each other. An increasing number of young husbands and live-in males are accepting the homemaking and childrearing roles on a part time or full time basis. Washing dishes, shopping, cleaning house, and the like, are being carried out quite successfully by many males. This takes them out of the competition for jobs or advancement in the marketplace. It provides a different type of satisfaction which may be supplemented further by a reflected joy in the achievements of the wife, plus the pleasures of being with the children. At the same time, there is an emphasis on the "macho" man in today's society. Movies involving karate, the achievements of Rambo, and Conan the Barbarian have been popular; John Wayne and Clint Eastwood movies are shown repeatedly; and TV shows about bravery in Vietnam, self-proclaimed vigilantes - like The Equalizer - and some "hard-nosed" private detectives are very popular. There is much interest in high-powered cars, carrying weapons, and an increased identification with college and professional football, boxing, and wrestling, all of which can be identified with power, strength, and force. There is an increased acceptance of homosexuality and bisexuality, but a continued desire for parenthood, both inside and outside of marriage. There is no question that a society may function with many diverse ways of life, but it is less certain that contradictory and conflicting patterns can continue indefinitely into the future. The current adult male population was generally reared within the same or compatible philosophies even though generational conflicts were increasing when they were in their teen years.

Ultimately, society may have to move toward a core type of male role in order to have a stable and workable rearing model for the male child. The young boy does not have the experience or maturity to know what a man is, or should be, if he is confronted with a continuing series of contradictions. If his father influences him in one direction, but his playmates and friends make fun of him and his father, his sexuality is not likely to achieve any real stability. The child is hurt and confused, but does not have a source to turn to who can resolve the differences. If the directions of male role behaviors continue to divide, there may finally be a polarization to the extent that one viewpoint and accompanying behaviors are categorically rejected by the other side. The consequence for the child is an absence of acceptance, except from those in the same camp. The problems for teachers, counsellors, and all those who work with children individually or collectively, become magnified and almost impossible to resolve. The child may not know why there is such confusion and anger around him, but he knows its there and he can't do anything about it.

A second trend centers around the female and the contradictions in the feminine roles. It is still a fact that only women can become pregnant, remain so for nine months, and then deliver a human child. This is true for the woman who believes she was created to be a wife and mother, but it is equally true for the most "liberated" woman who is college educated, career oriented, in the middle of the competition for advancement and recognition, and who is always willing to assert her rights as a person equal to others. Many young women have great difficulty in reconciling the requirements of motherhood with those of liberation, equality, and a career. The desire to be a mother becomes intermingled with disruptions that are occurring in her personal and professional lives. The pressure to stay home with a sick baby cannot easily be rationalized in relation to the pressure to attend an important meeting at the office. There is also the exhaustion from too much to do and the feeling of too little time in which to do it. The young woman who has no children, wants no children, and has no guilt feelings about her position, is not caught in these dilemmas, but such a person is not too common. It is quite feasible for a woman to avoid having children, it is more difficult to come to believe she shouldn't have them, and it is very hard to reject or deny the pressures from family, peers and friends to be a mother.

Perry

Six year old Perry was talking on the phone to his best friend, Tony, when his grandfather heard him ask, "Why do you have to help your father clean the house? I want you to come on over and play with me on the computer."

Later, Tony did come over and the two boys entered into a discussion about helping their parents around the house. Perry said, "I empty the wastebaskets and I help Dad wash the car, but I don't do the dishes or clean the house, That's girl's work." Tony replied angrily, "It is not only for girls. My Daddy stays home and cooks the meals and does the dishes and washes the clothes and all sorts of things around the house." Perry asked, "Why doesn't your mother do those things?" and Tony said, "Because she's an executive and she has an important job and she makes lots of money."

Perry's grandfather spoke up and asked, "Does your Dad have a job too?" and Tony told him that he didn't. He said, "My Daddy likes to stay home and take care of everything and get the dinner. He likes to take care of me and my mother likes to go to the office and work there." The grandfather commented that in his day, the men went to work and the women kept the house and took care of the children. He added that "Times sure have changed."

Note that Perry and Tony are aware of the differences in the sex roles in the two families, but they do not find one is good or bad. Perry's family pattern is much more common, but the house-husband is present to some degree in most communities. If the parents accept the pattern and make a good adjustment, children will accept it without a problem. It has been argued that many families may benefit from a reconsideration of their role arrangement, but not necessarily toward an egalitarian relationship (Cowan & Cowan, 1988). In cases where the husband cannot find a job or is an under-earner, but resents it, the child will be much more aware of the traditional sex roles and feel they are the more normal. If the father cooks the meals and does the dishes, the little boy may not want to help, but not because it is not proper. Any style of life will succeed if all the family members understand their place in it and the relationship of that place to all the others. Boys and girls are not automatically meant to do or be anything, but they can be taught a pattern and come to really believe it is the natural and right way to do things. This is a real boon for teachers of young children, but they have a responsibility to teach that which is compatible with the beliefs of the parents and also the larger society.

THE FACTOR OF AIDS

In 1979, a new disease surfaced in the United States, concentrated primarily among the male homosexual population. However, the Center for Disease Control did not start tracking the disease until 1981, and treatment was begun in the same year. This disease was given the name "Acquired Immune Deficiency Syndrome," but is generally known as "AIDS." When a person is sick with AIDS, he or she is in the final stages of a series of health problems caused by the HIV virus which is transmitted primarily through sexual contact or the sharing of intravenous drug needles. The number of Americans exposed to the virus is estimated at one million, and those who are infected or have died are almost 365,000. At this time, the disease of AIDS is not fully defined and neither effective treatment or cure is possible; prevention is the only effective approach today (Reed, 1988; Macklin, 1989). Research scientists say that a preventive vaccine is a distant solution at best.

There is more concern and fear about AIDS than any disease in recent history, because there is uncertainty as to how it may be acquired and because it results in a high degree of fatalities. Death is common because the disease damages the immunity of the body and permits serious diseases to develop in those afflicted that would not affect other persons. At present, to be diagnosed as an AIDS victim, a person must have a damaged immune system and have an officially recognized infection. The Public Health Service predicts that by the end of the first decade, 1991, AIDS will have afflicted 270,000, and further during the year 1992, 80,000 new cases will be diagnosed. They expect the total number afflicted to increase to 450,000 by 1993. Inasmuch as the AIDS virus is transmitted through body fluids, specifically semen and blood, those persons at highest risk are homosexual and bisexual men, I.V. drug abusers, hemophiliacs, people who had multiple blood transfusions between 1978 and 1985, plus any sexual partners of those in these categories.

In a current book by Masters, Johnson, & Kolodny (1988), the authors contend the risk among heterosexuals is much greater than previously thought. The relationship of AIDS to heterosexual contacts is not fully resolved in the minds of many who are studying the disease. The majority of victims so far have come from the high risk groups, but the nature and consequences of sexual behavior which crosses the lines among homosexual, heterosexual, bisexual, promiscuous, and other contacts has not been measured on any large scale. It has been estimated that 25 to 30 percent of those infected with the virus will develop AIDS; others develop a related, but rarely fatal syndrome called ARC (AIDS-Related Complex); and others will never experience the symptoms. However, anyone infected with the AIDS virus is capable of transmitting it to another person. This includes an infected mother passing it to her fetus during pregnancy, and to the child during birth. These may become less common as testing of pregnant women becomes more widespread.

The current testing program for AIDS is quite reliable and anyone who tests positive is considered infected with the virus. This means they are capable of transmitting the disease through the blood or in a sexual discharge, although they may or may not contract the disease itself. It is possible to be infected for years, feel fine, look fine and have no way of knowing you are infected, unless you are tested. The Public Health

Service recommends a person seek counselling and testing if he or she has ever engaged in any behavior that involves a risk of acquiring AIDS.

A current controversy centers around who should be tested and under what conditions. Mandatory testing has been proposed for food handlers, criminals, persons getting married, social workers and teachers, and a few have suggested the entire population. Most contend that it is unnecessary to test everyone, and that to do it for a few specified categories would be discriminatory. Even if certain groups to be tested could be agreed upon, there is the matter of compliance and the penalty for failure to do so. Such concerned persons, as the recent Surgeon General Everett Koop, are not pushing for mandatory testing; their primary emphasis is on education and voluntary testing centers. Widespread advertising about safe sex through the use of condoms, and the free distribution of condoms on college campuses and elsewhere are recent developments in the battle against AIDS. The free distribution of needles to drug addicts has also taken place, albeit not without argument. Sexual abstinence has been rejected by all but a few as being impractical for the public.

One of the significant byproducts of AIDS has been some real changes in the nature of the Sexual Revolution of the last thirty years. The free and open exchange of sexual partners practiced among many young people, both single and married, has slowed dramatically, and a very careful selection of partners is the practice. In the homosexual world, there is a substantial increase in sexual caution in both partners and practices. Concern has also expanded in the heterosexual world, because of the number who are bisexual and the fact that a number of husbands have been involved with prostitutes or casual liaisons. If any contacts are infected, the involved partner may contract the disease and may then infect future partners. One further consequence has been an emphasis on revealing any "secret life" to current and future sex partners. This occurs among both "straights" and "gays." The implications of AIDS for marriage, parenthood and children, in addition to sexual activities, can hardly be exaggerated.

AIDS AND CHILDREN

The incidence of AIDS in infants and small children is not great at present, but the potential for increase makes it of great concern. In 1988, more than 2000 small children were believed to have either AIDS or AIDS-related illnesses. The Public Health Service predicts the number will triple in less than four years. Ongoing research indicates that 30 to 50 per cent of infected mothers will pass the virus on to their children. Almost 80 per cent of the infected children contracted the virus in utero and most will die before their fifth birthday. The women at highest risk - including those who are drug users or living with IV drug users - are the least likely to seek an abortion or even be tested; most are poor, uneducated, and financially destitute. State laws often prevent children born to IV drug users from returning home with their mothers, so many of the children wind up in a foster home. The remainder live out their days in the hospital. All the children with AIDS suffer the pain, fear, and isolation common to the terminally ill, but many of them also are psychologically scarred because they have been abandoned.

One of the important consequences of AIDS, in addition to the infection itself, is the exposure of people, including the young, to publicity about causes and consequences. The young child is exposed to the public and private discussions about the sexual implications of the disease. One hears about homosexuality, intercourse, condoms, and other aspects of sex behavior which must create a sensitivity to the world of sexuality. Whether any of this contributes to an understanding of the child's own vague and undirected feelings is problematical, but surely an interest is established in the area. A disorganized curiosity is developed at an earlier age than was true in the past. It has been estimated by the Planned Parenthood Association that as many as 20,000 sexual scenes are shown on television each year. The young child will not see many of these and is not likely to have much interest in those that are seen. However, there is good reason to deal promptly and directly with any questions a child may ask about such scenes and their implications. For example, if a four year old boy sees open-mouth kissing, or an ad for condoms, and wonders about them, an honest, direct, but simple answer geared to the child's age and learning level is quite in order.

Parents normally make little or no effort to educate their children about sex and sex-related matters when they are small. There is no set guideline as to when to begin, but it is necessary to start sometime. Most experts believe that by the age of five, it is appropriate to establish a basic understanding of the body parts and their functions. Use the right names and explain that the body will change as they grow older. Develop a general understanding of where babies come from, some knowledge of male and female and the similarities and differences, and be prepared to answer questions about anatomical differences. In 1987, Education Secretary William Bennett and Surgeon-General Everett Koop issued a joint statement to the effect that education has a fundamental role in teaching young people how to avoid the threat of AIDS. Koop says that health and human development education should begin in kindergarten. Pre-school children may ask about AIDS - "What is it?", "How do you catch it?", "What can doctors and nurses do about it?" - just as they ask about other illnesses. For very young children, parents should focus on staying healthy, what it means to be sick, and the importance of following recommended treatments. All these considerations are important, but they must be explained in accordance with the maturity and awareness of the child. Thus, a child with an ailing grandparent living in the home will have a different grasp of illness and its complications than other children.

A frequent impact on a child who has AIDS, or even its presence in his family, is to be ostracized in school, on the playground and sometimes throughout the entire community. In some places, children have been denied the right to attend school while in others, parents keep their children home when the infected child is allowed to attend. In one community, the house in which several children who had AIDS lived was burned down during the night. When Ted Koppel, on his program, Nightline, asked a child with AIDS who his friends were, the young boy replied, "I don't have any friends." Later, when his family moved to another community, advance preparations were undertaken by the school and he was welcomed by the staff and the students, including the leaders. On occasion, children with AIDS will be in isolation because they are too ill to play outside or participate with other children in their daily activities. If a child is able to attend a child care center, Kindergarten, or other facility for young children, most schools are likely to grant admission; the courts have upheld such admissions regardless of complaints from parents of other children.

There are children currently attending school who are infected and the officials and teachers are unaware of it. It can be argued that this is dangerous because the child is exposed to diseases and infections for which he or she has little or no resistance and thus cannot be protected by the school system. In New York City, a panel evaluates the suitability of putting children with AIDS in regular classes. In Texas it is illegal to notify a teacher that a child has AIDS, unless his or her parents consent. Such policies are intended to protect the child from stigmatization, teasing, and to reduce community protests. Approaching the problem from a general health angle, the Center for Disease Control in Atlanta advocates that those caring for infants and children with AIDS use precautionary methods, including the use of gloves, plus great care when handling and disposing of body fluids and discharges, such as blood, urine, feces, vomit, and saliva. If teachers and nurses are unaware that a child is infected, they may not follow these recommendations, although the severity of the AIDS virus requires that common sense precautions be taken in all appropriate situations. However, the CDC also says that casual contact among persons, including school children, appears to pose no threat and children with AIDS should be allowed to attend school.

The American Academy of Pediatrics has agreed with the CDC that school age children should be allowed to attend school. There are only three exceptions: aggressive children who bite, children who can't control their bodily excretions, and children with open skin lesions. In June 1986, the city of Chicago adopted a policy on AIDS that covered school personnel, children in grades K-12, and pre-schoolers. The policy provided guidelines for handling bodily fluids, established guidelines for reporting cases, and allowed children to attend school unless medical and school officials and the child's parents agreed that alternative instruction was warranted. The general direction of policies established in recent years is increasingly in the direction of admission of the child with AIDS, but the matter of privacy is less well established. Some systems have announced that children with AIDS were attending school, but refused to identify the child or children. The major means of reducing tensions, protests, and the withholding of children from school seems to be educating the parents and the community as a whole about AIDS, its severity, and the restricted means by which it is possible to become infected. It is agreed that an infected child is entitled to an education and to the same love and attention that any other child receives.

Bradley, Lyle, and Angelo

Four year old Bradley grabbed the toy his four year old friend, Lyle, was playing with and started to play with it. Lyle grabbed it back and said, "You are bad to take my toy, and you are bad because you have AIDS." Brad retorted, "I am not bad. You're bad and you have AIDS too." Quickly, the two little boys went on to other things, the exchange of harsh words forgotten.

A few days later, three year old Angelo did not come to the nursery to play and the teacher told the children that he was very sick. The children went on to play and Lyle said, "Angelo must be real bad sick. I wonder if he will die?" Bradley answered, "I know you sometimes die when you have AIDS and don't get to be a grown-up." The other boy said, "I know what let's do - make Angelo a picture and have the teacher give it to him." Lyle and Bradley set to work immediately to prepare their gift for their young friend.

The three children just mentioned are patients in a special Children's AIDS ward in a major metropolitan hospital. Of the six children in the ward, four were born with AIDS, one contracted it from a blood transfusion, and one from being molested by an uncle who had the disease. These young people know they are sick from something called AIDS. They know that they can die from the disease, but the relation of hospitals, treatments, and doctors to their problems is not very meaningful. Neither is death. They accept each other fully and exhibit all the usual emotions and reactions of small children. They worry about each other and become very concerned when one of the group is unable to participate in their activities. Unfortunately, it is unlikely that any of these children will live very long. The nursery teacher must work very hard to make this limited time as rewarding as possible for these seriously ill children.

A nursery in a hospital for children with AIDS is unusual at the present time, but such programs may become common before too long. At one time it was thought that children would not be very much affected by AIDS, but that idea has been dissipated by the increase of the virus in young people from a variety of sources. As AIDS increases in the general population, the number of women with the disease who bear children will also increase, producing a substantial number of infants who are infected. Sexual child abuse by persons with AIDS has not decreased. All in all, it is predictable that the need for special programs for infants and small children will increase substantially in the near future. This means that programs for young children will have to come to grips with the question of how they will handle admissions and treatment of children with AIDS. School systems and hospitals around the country will also have to make decisions with regard to treatment, privacy, personnel assignments, and the serious questions related to publicity and public relations.

CARE FACILITIES FOR CHILDREN OF WORKING MOTHERS

A most significant social change in the last few decades has been the tremendous increase in the number of mothers of young children entering the work force. In the early stages of this movement, it was quite controversial, especially with regard to the impact of the separation of mother and child for several hours. Today, the major issue is the availability and quality of the facilities in which the child is placed while the mother is at work. In 1970, 24 percent of women with infants under one year of age were working outside the home, while in 1988, it was 52 percent, according to the Bureau of Labor Statistics. Almost two-thirds of the mothers who are single or alone and have children between the ages of three and five are employed. Furthermore, there is no sign that these trends are slowing down. In fact, both public and private schools are increasingly faced with the situation of children who have no one at home when school lets out each day.

A statement released at a recent "Day Care Summit" in Washington asserted that for both infants and toddlers, "there is every reason to believe that both the children and their families can thrive" when the parents, "have access to stable child care arrangements featuring skilled, sensitive, and motivated care givers." However, it is contended by many experts that the lack of affordable, quality care for young children has escalated to crisis proportions. In 1988, the Congress considered legislation entitled the "Act for Better Child Care Services" (ABC) and also a more modest Child Care Services bill. Both faced considerable opposition, partly for the expected increase in cost with each passing year, and partly because of questions as to the standards that should prevail. What should be the role of parents? What might be the relative responsibility of the Federal government in relation to the various states? According to child care lobbyists, the ability of states and municipalities has been stretched to the point where they cannot afford to support adequate child care programs, so the question of Federal financing for child care has increasingly become one of "what kind of support should it be?" Child care facilities can now be found in recreation centers, malls, churches, housing projects, government agencies, businesses and factories, in addition to those in schools and privately-owned and operated programs. According to Hofferth (1989), the cost today can be ten percent of the budget for a middle income family and as high as 26 percent for low income families. Parents are usually required to pay for the services, but there is also considerable subsidization by business, industry, and government. Efforts to train persons to be placed in the home to care for young children have generally been unsuccessful, partly because the cost to the parents is substantial, and partly due to a shortage of people for such programs.

To understand the full implications of child care, it is necessary to examine such factors as costs, facilities, transportation, and staff. The better the quality of the services provided, the greater the cost, so anything beyond mere custodial services begins to become quite expensive. At the present time, U.S. policy does not define or establish the standards of high quality infant, toddler, or pre-school child care. There is no uniformity nor consistency among those that do exist. Some feel that the Federal government should take full responsibility for creating and maintaining quality child care programs throughout the country. Others reject the idea, citing government control and/or the delays in funding legislation that may occur. Generally, the use of Federal funds for research and some form of subsidies for the poor and handicapped is acceptable, as is the establishment of an educational and informational service. During the 1980s, Federal child care funds were drastically reduced and most states also cut back on their funding, spending less than they did in the 70s. On the other hand, the need for child care support is steadily increasing, especially to assist young mothers who are striving to work their way out of poverty. It is estimated that two-thirds of all young children will have both parents in the work force by 1995. At present, more than 56 percent of children under six are cared for to some extent by someone other than their parents. The combination of these trends may well make child care a major political and corporate issue in the next decade. It may also become significant as a contract negotiation issue and as a fringe benefit for workers and employers, and indeed, for all employees.

According to Ellen Galinsky, Co-President of New York City's Family and Work Institute, 200 corporations currently have on-site child care facilities. This on-site service has the advantage of convenience, security, and sometimes, the opportunity for one or both parents to be with the child during rest breaks and the lunch period. Occasionally provisions will be made for the nursing mother to be with her baby periodically. It remains true, however, that the main characteristics of the work schedule have not changed in relation to a working mother's needs so that available time with the child is frequently "the luck of the draw," i.e., the nature of the job and its demands. As the pressure increases for more facilities and programs for working mothers, fundamental modifications in the structure of the work place will be in order. The extent to which changes can be made to accommodate both staff and line requirements and child care needs will need to be explored further.

The total number of companies that provide some form of child care is nearing 5,000. The most common approaches are child care resource referral to assist parents find facilities with flexible spending accounts, including a salary reduction plan that allows for payment with pre-tax dollars, flexible time-scheduling for parents, paid parental leave for mothers and fathers, and sick-child leave or released time. These approaches seem to represent a good financial investment for the company if they result in decreased employee turnover, boosts recruitment opportunities, and contributes to greater employee satisfaction with a resulting increase in production. While there will be disruptions and increased costs in the short run, the benefits of the child care facilities and/or programs will certainly be rewarding for everyone with the passage of time.

In addition to the industrial world, public school systems are becoming an important resource for on-site child care. Currently pre-school programs are funded or being developed in more than half of the states with expenditures totalling over 250 million dollars annually. One possibility is to use existing elementary school buildings for on-site child care programs, both before and after school for both pre-school and school age children.

In addition, full day care may be available during holidays and vacation periods. Furthermore, this system can be expanded to offer a family support center for first-time parents, a supportive program for private day-care homes in the neighborhood, and provide information and referral services. The ultimate authority rests with the school board and the immediate responsibility belongs to the elementary school principal. The program for the school children is normally under the supervision of child development personnel, headed by an Early Childhood educator. The staff might include some teachers from the regular staff, upper level college students in elementary education, retired teachers, and substitute teachers. The tax payers of the community finance the public school system and its facilities; the child care program is paid for primarily by fees from those who choose to use it. Such fees may be based on income and ability to pay, and may also be subsidized by government grants for those in need. Charges are usually higher for pre-school children in the program than for children who are already attending the school during the regular hours.

The nature and the location of child care facilities and the financial base of support are important for the establishment and maintenance of the program. A more critical test, however, is the well-being of the young child while he or she is not under the parents' care. Numerous studies have indicated a positive effect upon the child when placed in a good environment. Most parents and educators accept this view, but there are those who believe that only parents should care for their young children during the formative years. The bottom line today is that, rightly or wrongly, many children of all ages are going to be placed with a variety of people frequently and for prolonged periods; therefore, the primary concern is to provide the highest quality care within the limits of the parents' and the community's ability to provide support.

A quality child care program must include the following: First, the physical needs of the child should be met through rigid health and safety requirements, by buying and maintaining appropriate and sturdy equipment and supplies, and offering regular opportunities to use the equipment following established and publicized rules and regulations and under proper supervision. Nutritional needs, along with adequate rest and nap periods, should be planned and monitored. Special care related to the ages of the children must be maintained for eating and snacking times, for handling the food, and for toilet facilities. Provision must be made for necessary inoculations, for removing a sick or injured child from the group and, if necessary, from the premises, and a policy clarifying the conditions for a child's return after an illness.

Second, a fully qualified staff must be present - but the nature of these qualifications requires some discussion. The key person is the director who should be trained to work with children of different ages, to organize and direct other workers, develop and manage a budget, and relate to children, parents, and staff. The more competent the director, the greater the flexibility in developing the rest of the staff. Age, sex, and race of the staff are not critical factors, but some diversity of personnel is valuable for the children's learning experiences. A screening for sex offenses, history of violent behavior, and contagious disease is in order, as well as a record of previous experiences in the work place. It is important that nonprofessional child care givers be provided with opportunities to learn more about young children and how to work with them. Good working conditions, stable salary conditions with opportunities for increments, and guaranteed fringe benefits for both professional and nonprofessional staff, will help maintain a sound program with real continuity. Above all, the people employed in a child care center should love children, be able to relate to them, and be capable of handling the tantrums and demonstrations of immaturity that will occur almost every day (Phillips & Whitebook, 1986).

In addition to proper physical facilities and competent staff, a qualified child care facility will provide a program that is a positive force in each child's social and emotional development. There should be planned learning situations, the promotion of intellectual development, and respect for the entire learning process and those who contribute to it. Each child should develop a healthy sexuality in accordance with his abilities so that age, intelligence, and maturity are all taken into account. The program should enable a child to build a good feeling about himself, learn to relate to his peers and to adults, to substitute verbal behavior for physical behavior in situations of frustration and disappointment and, in general, learn the rules of life. Finally, a good child care center will work with the parents and the community to build an integrated world for a child and thus lay the foundation for the future.

It must be pointed out that there are some complications in the planning and operation of any child care program that will affect the well-being of a child. There are occasions when youngsters wish to stay at the center at the end of the day because it is cleaner, roomier, better equipped, and more pleasant than home. The young child may get better food, more attention, and there may be less bickering and conflict situations. There may also be a greater sense of security and of being wanted. One possible result is conflict between child and parent and even greater dissatisfaction at home. The young child does not have a good understanding of the reasons for the differences between the two settings, but does know that one seems more satisfying than the other. The staff must take great care not to accentuate or exploit this situation.

Another potential problem associated with the child care program is the pressure put on the mother, especially one without a partner, to prepare the child for the center, work all day, and take care of the child's needs in the evening. She may resent the extra demands put upon her, but she has to work, thus the child is caught in the middle. If the child dawdles in the morning, the mother becomes irritated. This is equally true if he or she is not ready to go home when she comes pick him up. If the child praises the facilities, the staff, the food, etc., at the center she may resent it or feel guilty or experience a sense of failure. Being tired from a long day, she may take it out on the child.

It is important that the child care program staff and the parents accept the fact that mothers work long days away from home, necessitating young parents to be away from their children, and that there are differences between the child care facilities and the home. These are all facts of life. They are nobody's fault. They will continue to exist. Consequently the greatest need is for mutual support, a reinforcement of the strengths of both, and for the child to feel loved and wanted in all settings. One study found that children with child care experience were less responsive to adults and more aggressive than children without such experience (Schenk & Gusec, 1986).

It is normal for parents to be concerned about the safety and well-being of their child when they are away from them. However, Galinsky & David, 1988, p. 365-66) write, "Children are not necessarily harmed or helped by the fact that their mothers are employed and they are cared for by others. The impact of the mother's employment depends; it depends upon the children's experiences in the families and in their child care situtations." On the other hand, concerns over day care may cause parents to be less productive and increase their absenteeism from the job, and can also have adverse affects upon their health. One concern that has increased dramatically in recent years is that of the child being sexually abused. Because of the wide-spread publicity of instances of child abuse in nurseries and pre-school programs, some factual and some not, many parents have become extremely worried that their child will be victimized. Child care centers can cope with these fears to a great extent by assuring the parents that the staff screening has been carefully done and the child is in the care of people who care. It is also important for a center to know where each child is and who he or she is with at all times. This is true from the time the child arrives at the facility until signed out to a parent or an agreed upon substitute at the end of the day. It is not impossible that child abuse will occur in fully licensed facilities, but it is reasonable to assume that there will be fewer incidents.

When parents need the services of child care facilities, it is appropriate to make arrangements to observe the available resources for a full day or more, and certainly during the time it is to be utilized by their child. Danger signals should arise if there is a reluctance to permit such visits or to deny any observations at any time. It is also recommended that the staff be met, their qualifications determined, and to learn their general orientation to a young child's social, emotional, physical, and intellectual needs. Small group activities along with well-chosen equipment are positive indicators. Licensing is required in all states, but there is real competition to get children into the best quality programs. From an economic point of view, public school programs are usually less expensive than privately owned ones, but the well-being of the child is always a primary consideration

In 1988, the National Child Care Staffing Study examined the quality of care in 227 child care centers in five metropolitan areas in the United States. The major findings centered around the importance of the child care teaching staff. The education of the staff, the wages they are paid, the nature of their work environment, and the staff-child ratio, were found to be determinants of the quality of services children receive. The suggested recommendations include: raising salaries, promoting educational and training opportunities, adopting state and federal standards to raise overall quality, and developing industry standards to minimize the disparities between types of child care programs. It was noted that, compared to a decade ago, child care centers receive fewer governmental funds, are more likely to be on a for-profit basis, and care for more infants (Whitebook, Howes, Phillips, & Pemberton, 1989).

A list of accredited early childhood programs can be obtained from the National Academy of Early Childhood. Write to the National Academy of Early Childhood Programs, 1834 Connecticut Avenue, N.W., Washington, D.C., 20009, or you can call (202) 232-8777 or 1 (800) 424-2460.

QUESTIONS FOR DISCUSSION

1. How does the change in the sex roles of men and women affect the ability of young children to learn their own roles? Is there more or less confusion in defining what it means to be male or female?

2. What are the responsibilities of a teacher who has a child with AIDS in the group? How does he or she protect the other children?

3. How would you cope with a young child with AIDS who bites? Who falls and receives a cut?

4. How would you handle the concerns of parents whose children are in a class with a child who has AIDS?

5. What are the major factors in developing a Child Care Center of high quality? How does different levels of quality affect the sexual development of young children who attend?

6. Define AIDS and HIV.

CHAPTER REFERENCES

Cowan, C.P. & P.A. Cowan (1988). Who does what when partners become parents: implications for men, women, and marriage. Marriage and Family Review, 12: 105-131.

Galinsky, E. & J. David (1988). The preschool years: family strategies that work - from experts and parents. New York: Times Books.

Hofferth, S. (1989). What is the demand for and supply of child care in the United States? A public policy report. Young Children, 44: 28-33.

Leslie, G.R. (1979). The family in social context. 4th ed. New York: Oxford University Press.

Macklin, E.D. (1989). AIDS and families. Marriage and Family Review, 13: 1-271 (Nos. 1 and 2).

Masters, W., V. Johnson & R. Kolodny (1988). Crisis: heterosexual behavior in the age of AIDS. New York: Grove Press.

Neal, A.G., H.T. Groat & J.W. Wicks (1989). Attitudes about having children: a study of 600 couples in the early years of marriage. Journal of Marriage and the Family, 51: 313-327.

Phillips, D. & M. Whitebook (1986). Who are the child care workers? Young Children, 41: 14-20.

Reed, S. (1988). Children with AIDS. Phi Delta Kappan (Special Repiort), 69: (No. 5) K1-K12.

Schenk, V.M. & J.E. Gusec, (1986). A comparison of prosocial behavior of children with and without day care experience. Merrill-Palmer Quarterly, 32: 231-240.

Whitebook, M., C. Howes, D. Phillips, and C. Pemberton (1989). Who cares? Child care teachers and the quality of care in America. Young Children, 45: 41-45.

CHAPTER VII

EMERGING AND CONTINUING ISSUES FOR THE FUTURE

This chapter is devoted to topics that are relatively undeveloped, sometimes controversial, often emotional, and some are quite technical; but they all are deserving of discussion, evaluation, and exploration with regard to their implications for infants and children. The relation of the topics to young children is not always direct and may sometimes seem out of the mainstream of developing sexuality, but they are nevertheless significant because of an impact on factors that do affect the environment or climate in which children are created, born, and reared.

It can be anticipated that young children will hear such terms as abortion, fetus, gays, AIDS, test tube baby, artificial insemination, and other current phenomena in the news. It is equally likely that they will meet children in child care facilities and kindergartens who are from one-parent families, or are homeless in a sense, or carry a house key, or children whose parents work at the same time of day. If a teacher is familiar with these and other situations described in this book, he or she can be comfortable with questions or comments from the children. While young children can be answered with honesty and respect, albeit on a rather elemental level, this is not the case when working with parents or guardians. Parents may advise their teachers of existing or impending problems that could have an impact on their children. They may also ask questions or seek guidance if they feel the teacher is well informed about the many aspects of sexual development. Finally, it is important to follow the developments in the various areas over a period of time, because they reflect ongoing attitudes about sex, children, and child-rearing.

BABIES, BABIES - TIMES ARE CHANGING

In the United States at the present time, half a million teenaged girls are having babies each year and a substantial number are poorly prepared to be effective mothers. In addition, a million and one-half women have abortions each year because they do not wish to become mothers, a preference which exists for a variety of reasons. In contrast, there are large numbers of couples who desperately desire to have children but have been unable to conceive them. Then there are the millions of couples who do want children, plan for them, and proceed to have them with a minimum of problems.

Figure 7-1 Photo courtesy of Marie Caracuzzo

The number of people in the last category is indicated by birth statistics, but the number of people in the others can only be derived from projecting from interviews, case studies, and the like. There are tens of millions of people who do not have children because of some type of infertility, meaning they have tried to have children for more than a year without success. Until recently, infertility has been most commonly associated with older women who delayed marriage or child-bearing for financial, health, or career reasons. While there are many such instances in the population, there are also many women with physical reasons that prevent conception. It is true that the number of infertile men is much greater than was once believed. More competent and thorough research also indicates that infertility is more common and increasing among young women from the age of twenty upward. Included among the explanations for the apparent increases in infertility are such factors as Sexually Transmitted Disease (STD), primarily among younger women, and endometriosis, which may occur at any age. The most common causes of STD are gonorrhea and chlamydia. The symptoms of gonorrhea are severe enough that victims usually contact doctors for help, but chlamydia often develops with virtually no symptoms. Both diseases, if untreated, can easily lead to infertility by causing infection in the uterus, fallopian tubes, and/or ovaries. Endometriosis may cause severe menstrual cramps, pelvic pain, very difficult sexual intercourse, increased bleeding, or there may be no really noticeable symptoms. Doctors believe the disease can cause subtle changes in crucial hormone production or block ovulation, thus resulting in infertility. Endometriosis can cause irreparable damage to the reproductive organs if not diagnosed early, but it is one of the most treatable causes of infertility.

In a small percentage of the cases of infertility, the cause cannot be identified. It has been suggested that excessive exercise which reduces the proportion of a woman's body fat may inhibit ovulation. Stress is mentioned as a factor in infertility as is the "environment," i.e., smog, noise, smoke, etc., all of which may affect the supply of estrogen. Some women have vaginal or cervical mucous which prevents the male partner's sperm from entering the uterus.

The use of fertility drugs has become a common resource to reduce infertility when other methods have failed. When couples are placed on these drugs, they are also advised that multiple births are a common consequence. In such cases, often highly publicized, the delivery is usually Caesarean and the babies are small. There are several problems associated with multiple births that have not been publicized. The chances of all the babies in a multiple birth being healthy are not good and the doctor may recommend that one or more of the fetuses be terminated. This is known as selective termination, not abortion, because the pregnancy continues if one or more of the fetuses continues to survive. An unusual example of selective termination occurred in 1988, in Ohio when the use of ultra-sound revealed nine sacs. A specialist determined that one fetus was already lost and the mother was about to miscarry. Two fetuses with the greatest chance of living were selected and the remaining six were terminated. The selection was based on the location in the womb which provided the best chance for continued growth and nourishment. These twins were born prematurely; one weighed five pounds and the other three. Both spent a month in intensive care and are surviving at last reports.

Male infertility is estimated to be the cause of half of all childlessness and, as might be expected, research on causes and treatment is underway with considerable success. One cause is distended veins which transfer heat to the testicles and kill the sperm. This can be treated by vein repair or by removing some arteries which permit proper blood flow to and from the penis.

Impotency, or the inability of the male to maintain an erection for intercourse, can be treated by a penile implant which produces the necessary rigidity. A more recent technique is the injection of medication into the penis which results in a dilation of the arteries and an increase in the blood flow and ultimately an erection. Some recent experimentation has been done with a manipulation of hormones to effect changes in the sperm production in the testicles. Male infertility can be treated by surgery in some cases. At least half of male problems with infertility can be corrected by these approaches, plus a change of lifestyle for some.

Couples who have one or more children and desire more may experience what has been called "secondary infertility," a failure to conceive again. Experts suggest that the risk factors for fertility increase with age, and all of the above-mentioned factors will be valid even after having children. Many couples in this situation seek to adopt additional children, but the fact that they have one or more biological children of their own sometimes weighs against them. The desire to avoid having an "only child" is a motivating force, as is a desire to have a boy or a girl if one sex is not present among the existing siblings.

Artificial Insemination and In Vitro Fertilization

One of modern medicine's most interesting and challenging frontiers is the treatment of fertility. Failure to have children has been of concern to people throughout recorded history and contributed to divorce, separation, accusations, feelings of guilt, adoption, as well as a myriad of substitute behaviors. As the knowledge of the process of fertilization and the reproductive process increased, efforts to improve parents' chances of having offspring have intensified and been increasingly successful. One of the most effective techniques in recent years has been artificial insemination. There are several variations, all of which are normally successful, although with degrees of controversy surrounding each.

In some cases, the wife is fully capable of becoming impregnated and carrying a child to full term, but the husband is infertile, at least to the degree that pregnancy does not occur after a reasonable period of trying. One of the most common techniques to achieve pregnancy is to use a substitute male donor for sperm which is then implanted into the wife's egg surgically. The selection of a donor may be done by the patient or a physician, or the sperm may be taken from a Sperm Bank. In either case, there is a careful screening to match the donor's characteristics with those of the husband, insofar as possible. This procedure creates a child who has the mother's genes and those of a male donor. Some husbands approve of the idea of their wife becoming pregnant and having a child even though they are not going to be the biological father. There is need for professional counselling in such cases to clarify the significance of the relationships for all concerned, especially the future definition of the father and child relationship without recrimination. Desire for a child and willingness to participate are not sufficient: emotional stability, soundness of the marriage, attitudes toward parenthood, plus the economic ability to provide for the well-being of a child are also basic requirements. One additional consideration in some instances of artificial insemination is the presence of genetic factors in one or the other of the parents that should not be transmitted to the child.

All of these conditions are equally applicable to another version of artificial insemination, namely, in vitro fertilization (IVF). First achieved successfully in 1978, IVF consists of fertilizing the wife's egg with the husband's sperm outside the body of the female. Although it is not available or affordable for most, about 3,000 babes have been born this way through 1987. The use of IVF occurs in cases where the husband's sperm is relatively weak or is low in count, but the wife ovulates normally. If the sperm, obtained by masturbation, fertilizes the egg in a glass container in the laboratory, the resulting embryo is transferred to the woman's uterus in two or three days. At the present time, the success rate of IVF is over 10 percent, although it may be repeated to improve the chances of fertilization.

For more than ten years, the question of what to do with extra embryos has existed and has not really been faced. It is normal to take several of a woman's embryos and freeze them (Cryopreservation). They are then stored to permit additional attempts at fertilization in case it becomes necessary. In a recent divorce case, the wife desired to continue attempts to become pregnant with implanted embryos; the husband was suing for joint custody (with the wife) over seven unused embryos, plus an assurance that nothing will be done with them, except by mutual agreement. In late 1989, a judge ruled that the embryos are the property of the wife, but further decisions are certain to be issued. It is estimated that in 1989 there are over 4,000 frozen embryos in the United States, but this is the first legal decision as to how they should be defined. The Roman Catholic Church, among others, has opposed their destruction, considering them as being comparable to any embryo or fetus and, therefore, human beings. Further unanswered questions are related to situations where one partner to an agreement dies, or one has a change of heart at some later date.

There are several alternatives to IVF, such as Gamete Intrafallopian Transfer (GIFT). This involves the surgical removal of eggs from a woman's ovary, mixing them with the husband's sperm, and replacing them back in the tubes where natural fertilization takes place. This procedure is less expensive than IVF and can be completed more quickly. A still newer procedure, Intrauterine Insemination (IUI), involves hormonal stimulation of the ovaries, plus a placing of the sperm in the uterus, thus bypassing the cervix. Obviously, decisions regarding the ownership and ultimate use of eggs and/or embryos remain unanswered, but are extremely important for the future of child-bearing.

Medical science has worked continuously on the techniques of treating infertility and the approaches just discussed are some of the results to date, the problem is a much more complicated one. The Roman Catholic Church, through the Vatican, has condemned all practices such as artificial insemination, in vitro fertilization, and surrogate motherhood, even if the husband and wife are the only ones involved. Many legislators, doctors, and clergymen are concerned to a high degree, and others are categorically opposed to research on human fetuses. Federal funds are prohibited from funding such research. On the other hand, many individual clergy, Roman Catholic and those of many other faiths, do not find all forms of aiding a couple with the problems of infertility unacceptable. Hospitals and universities with religious affiliations are caught in a dilemma which intermingles desire for knowledge, the methods of the research scientist, and ethical viewpoints, which are not always compatible. Most parents who want children and have not been able to conceive are not receptive to religious, moral, or legal restrictions. Nevertheless, there are no guidelines from state or the federal government, so a number of clinics are performing fertilization services for couples who can afford them, but there is a real danger that some are not fully responsible nor is the supervision as good as it might be.

A different situation exists, no less easily resolved, in a few cases wherein the seeker of fertilization is an unmarried couple or even a single, unattached woman. It can be anticipated that the number of such persons wanting to be parents will increase rapidly as the techniques described, as well as new developments, become more available and less expensive. It should be kept in mind that there are no established standards for becoming parents, so these people have a right to pursue their wishes unless it is legislated against in the future.

Finally, it should be noted that all the techniques discussed are most successful when the parents-to-be are young, inasmuch as effectiveness declines with age. When one considers the high cost, the current attempts at helping persons with their fertility needs are mostly limited to young, financially stable couples who may not be the ones most in need of such assistance.

Genetic Research, Amniocentesis, and Fetal Transplants

It may seem that genetic scientists live in a dream world far from reality and that their goals are not of science fiction, but the fact is that their logic is not only challenging, but understandable, and potentially attainable. If the genetic organization of man can be established, the long run consequence could well be an ability to identify the function of each gene and, ultimately, the possibility of replacing those that are defective or dysfunctional. Each person has approximately 100,000 genes, each of which serves a purpose, i.e., one contributes to the color of the eye, another to the nail on the little finger, and yet another to the testes of a male child. For each individual, the genetic organization is unique, making him or her not only what he or she is, but also distinct from anyone else. The genes are arrayed along twenty-three pairs of chromosomes, and an individual's organization is repeated in every cell in his body. At this time, there has been some progress in establishing the organizational sequences of genes along the chromosomes. This approach is directed toward providing a map of the order and function of these genes through the human body. Some of the chromosomes related to genetic diseases are pretty well mapped and the entire process may be only a few years away from completion.

A decade ago, only a handful of genetic diseases were able to be detected; now it is possible to identify 200 such diseases, often within eight weeks after conception. Unfortunately, with a few exceptions, they cannot be cured and there are very limited treatments available. The detection of these genetic problems has been facilitated to a high degree by the development of a procedure called amniocentesis. This involves the extraction of some of the amniotic fluid which surrounds the fetus in the womb. It is carried out by inserting a hypodermic syringe through the abdominal wall. From this fluid, it can be determined whether the fetus is that of a boy or a girl, whether the child is retarded or crippled, and whether there is a major genetic disease present.

In recent years, researchers have been able to identify such diseases as Duchennes Muscular Dystrophy, Cystic Fibrosis, Huntington's disease, and retinoblastoma, by testing the amniotic fluid. In addition, links to Alzheimer's disease and manic-depression have been found. These and other genetic diseases are responsible for twenty percent of the deaths of newborn children, contribute to fifty percent of miscarriages, and are responsible for eight out of ten cases of mental retardation.

Amniocentesis may be performed in any situation, but is most often employed in cases where the pregnant woman has a history of genetic disease in her family or is over thirty-five years of age. The risk of genetic disease is significantly greater for the child when born to women in these categories. The test is conducted when the fetus is about sixteen weeks old. A more recent test known as CVS can be used when the fetus is only 9 to 11 weeks old, but it involves greater risk to the fetus, although less to the mother. The results can be obtained in one to two weeks, sooner than with amniocentesis. If the results are negative, this permits earlier counselling and decisions about the future. The CVS procedure has been performed over 35,000 times worldwide and is considered an acceptable alternative to amniocentesis.

Although they are not common, complications can arise from the use of amniocentesis. These include a continued bleeding or leakage of the amniotic fluid, injury to the placenta or fetus, and miscarriage. However, if there is reason to suspect genetic problems, amniocentesis and CVS are effective procedures to determine the nature of the problem. Some time in the future, the decision as to what to do if genetic defects are found to exist in the fetus may be simplified, but at present it is a very complicated one. In fact, the severity of the decisions that may arise from amniocentesis and CVS causes many medical professionals to discourage their use for the determination of the sex of the fetus in order to make judgments related concerning the future of the pregnancy. Generally, this is considered a poor use of such an important test and, for some, borders on the unethical. It might be noted here that there is an unproven and controversial method for choosing the sex of a child prior to conception. Based on the fact that the sperm that will result in a male child is heavier than that for a girl, sperm can be selected and employed by artificial insemination to produce the desired result. Success rates are estimated at 80-85 percent for a male and 70-75 percent for a female. However, this procedure is very restricted with one physician franchised in each state to carry it out for a fee.

Returning to the consequences of negative findings from a test for genetic diseases, there are essentially three directions that one might follow: allow the defective fetus to be born and prepare the parents for the problems and needs in caring for the child; attempt transplants or other corrective actions for the defects or deficiencies in the child's organs or tissues; or thirdly, terminate the pregnancy. A genetically defective child often has a very short life expectancy and its activities are severely limited during that period. The medical expenses, requirements for care and attention, and extremely limited range of social behaviors are very trying for all parents, but especially for those who are unaware of the nature of genetic diseases. Often, after a period of trying very hard to take care of the child, he or she still must be institutionalized by the parents. On the other hand, there are instances in which the child lives at home, is provided with love and affection, and the parents and other siblings cope with the problems and needs quite well. (See Figure 7-2) The major concerns are the substantial cost of caring for the child and meeting his or her medical needs, plus the physical and mental strain of dealing with a difficult situation that is unlikely to ever get better and may gradually become worse. In some cases, there is an added burden of guilt feelings, based on the idea that the parents did something wrong or failed to do something right.

Figure 7-2 Photo courtesy of Diane Wilson

The second alternative for facing the discovery of a genetically defective fetus is to try to do something about it. Certainly the transplanting of hearts, livers, eyes, and other organs has been generally accepted as a means of helping people who have a defective or failing organ. This help means replacing the bad organ with a good one from someone who can do without it. There have been two sources until recently, a deceased person who agreed, or his family did, to donate his organ after death, and a living person who has two of some organ and is willing to provide one of them to someone else, often a family member. These sources have been utilized with increasing frequency and with greater success each year. The major limitation to organ transplants has been a shortage of available organs at the time needed, because there is a limit on the time for removal of an organ from one person and the placing in another. It also requires special conditions and personnel. In the last few years, a new source of organs and also tissues which has great possibilities from the standpoint of medical researchers and physicians has been found, namely, human fetuses that have been aborted. Some doctors have already begun to use fetal tissue for cases involving neurological diseases, e.g., Alzheimer's disease, Huntington's disease, and epilepsy. One reason for the activity in this direction is that the probability of rejection is less for fetal tissue because it is immature and thus more adaptable. In addition, the vitality of these young cells may be employed for such achievements as the establishing of new nerve connections in order to improve memory, restore sight in the blind, and even provide normal genes to fetuses found to have sickle-cell anemia or hemophilia. In West Germany recently, surgeons have transplanted fetal kidneys into three patients. In Mexico, fetus tissue was grafted into the brain of two Parkinson's disease victims who improved dramatically.

In addition to aborted fetuses as a source of organs and tissue, a recent development involves anencephalic children who are born without most of their brain. These infants normally die promptly after birth, but it was recently reported that three such children were being kept alive by the use of respirators in order to use their organs for transplantation. The respirators prevent the deterioration of the organs after birth by maintaining a steady supply of oxygen to the child until the transplant is carried out. There are about 3,500 anencephalic babies born in the United States each year. Most of the brain is missing, although there is a brain stem. Such a condition is usually identified during the fifth month of pregnancy. Among the infants carried to term, 60 percent die in a day and 97 percent die within a week.

In 1987, an infant called Baby Paul received medical and media attention when he was implanted with a heart from an anencephalic baby who died shortly after birth as the brain stem began to fail. The major attention was on the nature of the donor, rather than the recipient, because of moral and ethical implications. In fact, the use of organs and tissues from aborted and anencephalic sources has become involved in the controversy over abortion. Some persons take the position that there should be a ban on the sale of fetal tissue, that women who are aborted should have no voice in the utilization of the tissues from their fetus, and no policy should promote the life of one over another. As one can imagine, the proposals for the dispersal of fetal tissue are often quite bizarre, including one from a woman who wanted to use her own fetus as a means of treating her own disease. Researchers are in agreement that the use of fetal tissue should be determined only in centers that are noted for their expertise in basic and clinical research. Even so, there is a great deal of conflict between humanitarian, medical research, and moral and ethical viewpoints.

PARENTS, PARENTS - WHAT IS A PARENT?

What is a parent? Who can be a parent? These may seem like silly questions, but try to answer the following: Does a child who is born to one couple, reared by another couple, and then adopted by a third couple, have two, four, or six parents? If a woman does not know which of several men impregnated here, is the one who did the father, even though she may ultimately decide that it was another man? Who are the parents when a surrogate is impregnated by sperm from a bank and the resulting child is reared by an unrelated couple? Complex questions such as these can be and are raised, and the answer may be influenced by religious beliefs, legal perspective, and/or social conscience. In given situations, there may be a biological father, a legal father, and/or a de facto father for an individual child.

Questions related to parenthood most often arise in situations of divorce and remarriage, in case of adoption, or in instances where a child has been abandoned and the role of parents has been assumed by persons with no blood relationship to the child, although they may have a legal status. Courts are often called upon to make decisions about monetary and support considerations which can affect love, emotions, and personal beliefs.

The United States Government and those of several states have rarely determined who can be a parent or even the circumstances in which someone can be considered a parent. Love, marriage, the desire to be a parent, and the willingness to be a parent are not necessarily critical in this area. Through blood tests, it has been possible to determine that a given man is not a father of a child, but not who the father is. More sophisticated testing is now closing in on identification of the actual father by the testing of a person's DNA, which are strands of genetic material that are miniscule human blueprints. DNA exists in every nucleus-containing cell in the body. It can be obtained from semen, from blood, or a full strand of hair, and cannot be denied. This is important primarily for legal purposes, especially for the assignment of financial support and the provision of a home for the child. The biological parents, the man who contributes the sperm and the woman whose egg is fertilized, are the sources for the genetic traits of the child and contribute a combining of qualities that have never existed before in a person. In the sociological sense, the adults who rear the child are the parents in the child's daily life, but they must work with the biological qualities that have been inherited, and over which they have no control.

No matter how an approach to parenthood is developed, there are some limitations. Obviously maturity and fertility are the prerequisites for biological parenthood. For most males, these come with puberty and continue indefinitely. For the female, they may occur well before the teens and normally terminate before the age of fifty. If a parental determination is made by the courts, social maturity, an acceptable life style, and some financial resources are usually considered, although specific requirements are not spelled out in law. From a social perspective, a parent provides food, shelter, clothing, attention, love, guidance, and many other things - but - the child must accept and treat that person as a parent. Many children are able to live with one man as "daddy" and spend time visiting another "daddy" without finding it difficult or unusual. The person who provides certain functions and needs for a child is the parent for the situation.

With regard to the focus of this book, the persons around the child are the key influences on the development of his or her sexuality. Whether a person is called "mommy" or "Mary" is really irrelevant. The woman who provides the essentials of daily living is serving as the mother in the child's thinking. At the same time, many children think of their biological parents as their "real" father and mother, even though they may not know them.

It is the person in charge in each given situation who determines the people with whom a child comes into contact. That is the "parent" who interprets both the small and the large environment in which Johnny or Susie are located and where they will grow up. For most children, there is only one set of adults who serve as parents while they are young, but having only one parent or a steadily changing set of adults does not restrict the role nor limit the importance of parents. Teachers can anticipate many situations and cope with them if they are well informed about the parental status with regard to their students.

In the last few years, milk cartons have been covered with pictures of children whose location is unknown; most are believed to be with an adult (often a parent) who does not have the legal approval to rear them. In the next three section, there is a discussion of categories of persons who function as parents but do not fit the more traditional definitions. Among these to be discussed are surrogate mothers who have children but don't act as parents, gay or single parents who are not a father and mother combination, homeless families who lack a residence, and latchkey kids who often serve as parents for their siblings for periods of time each day.

Surrogate Mothers

Generally, if a woman agrees to become impregnated and then carry the resulting fetus to term for another woman, and then give the child to that woman, she is known as a surrogate mother. This situation arises when a couple wants a child and, for whatever reason, are unable to have one, they decide to contract with some woman who receives the husband's sperm, bears the child, and is paid an agreed-upon amount to then deliver the child to the contracting couple. Surrogate motherhood is not a new phenomenon, but it has received a lot of attention and a number of legal and sociological questions have been raised because of a case in which a surrogate decided she wished to keep her child. The woman who carried Baby M, as the child was identified in newspaper accounts, had signed a contract and been paid a fee to bear and deliver the child. Her refusal to deliver the child to the contracting couple raised serious questions about the adequacy of the law to deal with contracts involving relationships as emotional as parenthood. The traditional concepts of mother and father lose a degree of meaning. To a lesser degree, similar questions have occurred in the past when a mother who had given up her child for adoption decided she wanted it back. In those cases and in the case of the surrogate mother, issues concerning the rights of the biological mother, the biological father, the legally adopting parents, even the rights of visitation by all concerned have gone to court for resolution. In terms of the dissatisfaction expressed by the "losing side" in all the cases decided so far, the existing statutes were not written with these kinds of relationships in mind.

The primary focus to date has been on (a) the legal aspects of contracts, payments, and the rights of the concerned adults, (b) on the emotional aspects of the woman bearing the child and giving it up versus the planning, anticipation, expenses, and rights of the couple who contract for a child and run into legal and social conflicts, and (c) on the social considerations of those agencies making arrangements to provide social services for a fee. One critic suggests it might be possible to establish a group of "breeder women" who would bear children for others for a fee. Others feel this is too close to the animal husbandry practices in the breeding of various farm and racing animals, and is totally unacceptable as a practice for human beings. The widely divergent viewpoints on surrogate motherhood are derived from religious differences in its interpretation, legal definitions of ownership, political concerns and needs for appropriate laws, and social concerns for social policies among the participants.

The authors suggest that probably the most important consideration should be the welfare of the child, with special emphasis on his or her growth and development into adulthood. If a baby is shifted back and forth between the biological parent and the contractual parent, and is called by different names in different social settings, does the child really have a chance to know who it is, what it is, and where it belongs? If a healthy sexuality is based on attitudes, experiences, and relationships, what are the consequences if the people who are rearing the child are in conflict, call each other names, and give the child different answers to its questions? If a teacher should encounter a child who is involved in any of the situations described above, she or he is not in a position to take sides or make judgments. The teacher is in a position to stabilize the sexual development of the child during the time he or she is under the supervision and responsibility of the program. It is also possible for the teacher to protect the child to some extent if there has been extensive publicity or a court case is ongoing or pending.

Gays As Parents

Every child has a biological father and mother, but this does not necessarily mean there are two parents in his or her life. Many young children have been reared by one parent, usually the mother, because of the death of the other parent or a divorce. In lower income groups, there have been many instances of abandonment, by the father in most cases. The source of the one-parent situation will result in differing atmospheres in which a child will be reared. The death of a parent may create sentimentality or idealism about the deceased, or there may be excessive sadness or even morbidity. Divorce can lead to hostility so the child experiences a lot of bitterness and negativism, including antagonism toward marriage and resentment of children. In cases where the father has walked out, the family may be too destitute to be concerned with anything except survival. In any case, the person rearing the child has to play the role of the absent parent as well as their own.

As the life styles of homosexuals has been increasingly publicized, both state lawmakers and the general public have become aware that children in our society are being reared with many different sexual orientations in the homes. Because states do not keep records on sexual preferences, the number of homosexuals who have adopted children is not known. Data on children who have been assigned to a homosexual person after a divorce are not available either. A few states have passed laws to forbid adoptions by homosexuals, and some forbid foster home placements. On the other hand, spokespersons for various gay, lesbian, and civil rights groups claim that there is increasing interest among homosexuals to adopt children and rear them. There is also interest among lesbians to become impregnated and have their own babies. This can be accomplished through artificial insemination, and informal networks have sprung up to find sperm donors for interested women. There are also a substantial number of homosexuals who have been a father or a mother in a marriage that subsequently broke up, perhaps because of the sexual orientation of one partner, who are currently rearing one or more children (Schulenberg, 1985).

In today's society, homosexuals face two substantial problems when seeking to adopt or obtain custody of children through agencies or the courts. A recent obstacle is the association of the disease AIDS with the gay population. The general uncertainty about how the disease can be transmitted has led to widespread community prejudice to allowing gays to take care of children in their homes. More knowledge about AIDS plus progress in prevention and treatment should reduce the severity of this problem. The second problem is more complex and, therefore, more difficult to resolve. Stated simply, many people believe that a child growing up in a home with one or more gay persons will be predisposed toward homosexuality. This generalized concern has aroused intense public policy debates, reflecting what some call legitimate fears for children's welfare and what others call myths and prejudices against homosexuals. Civil liberties groups and gays rights organizations say no one should be denied the chance to raise a child solely because of sexual orientation. Those who have reviewed a number of research projects which compared two groups of children - one reared by lesbian mothers, the others by single heterosexual mothers - assert that no major differences were found. It was found that the children raised by lesbians showed nothing unusual in gender identity development, no greater preference for homosexuality and no serious social or emotional maladjustments (Bozett, 1987).

A young child living in the home of a gay man will be aware that there are women called mothers in the homes of children in the neighborhood, but that will be accepted. If the gay parent has a steady lover, the child may be exposed to two "daddys." If the home contains two lesbians, the child lives with two "mommies." The young child is aware of the differences between one home and another, but the significance of the differences will only be meaningful to the extent that they are pointed out and defined by playmates and neighbors (Green, 1978).

Singles As Parents

Singles as parents exist for one of two reasons; one of the partners in a marriage with one or more children is no longer in the home, or an unmarried person has assumed the responsibility for rearing one or more children. There are several substantial differences for the development of a child between the two sets of circumstances. The married person without a partner may or may not have to share visitations, may or may not have some kind of financial arrangement with the absent spouse, may or may not be the parent of some or all of the children, and may or may not have two sets of grandparents to relate to. The children are defined as legitimate and support from the families, relatives, and neighbors will likely be positive. As mentioned above, there may be some substantial attitudinal variations among cases involving divorce, separation, and death.

In the case of the unmarried person with children, the situation may be the result of either wanted or unwanted pregnancies. The decision to have the child and rear it may have been made completely voluntarily because the child was wanted, or it may have been made under considerable duress from others. The unmarried mother faces a number of potential problems, including dating and marriage (some men don't want a ready-made family), employment and the necessity to make arrangements for the child, as well as appropriate housing, available schools, coping with illness of the child or herself, and the existence of negative attitudes toward unmarried mothers on the part of people in the neighborhood or workplace.

Those who work with young children usually become quickly aware of each child's home situation from the conversations with other children and also remarks to adults. The presence of one or more children from homes with gay or single parents will not necessarily call for any specific attention on the part of the teacher or worker (Briggs & Walters, 1985). In some cases, there may be name-calling on the part of some children, or critical views from parents of other children in the group. It is the teacher's responsibility to stop this and protect the child from becoming upset or hurt. Children from such homes are normally quite comfortable with one parent, as that is all they have ever known. Perhaps the most serious situations arise when the parent becomes involved in a conflict with another person and the child is caught in the middle. The teacher may find it necessary to make sure the child is picked up by the authorized person at the end of the day, or is not disturbed during the day. Messages sent home with the child or by mail should be addressed appropriately and a follow-up may be in order. At the same time, the teacher must be careful to avoid involvement in conflict situations and must not take sides. The child needs to be protected and may require special attention during crisis periods. Generally, however, children with one parent, whatever the reason, can be integrated into any group without problems. The development of the sexuality of these children will be comparable to and indistinguishable from that of the other children. One study found some differences in awareness of male and female stereotypes between children from one and two parent families, but no differences in gender identity (Brenes, Eisenberg & Helmstadter, 1985).

Homeless Families

The helplessness of the human offspring and the number of years required to reach maturity is unique in the animal world. Newly hatched fish promptly swim; birds can peck or fly in hours or days; calves and colts stand up, nurse, graze, and move about almost immediately after birth; while the human baby lies in a bed for months, waving arms and legs aimlessly. While animals rely primarily on instincts and reflexes, humans require learning. Today, a minimum of sixteen years is involved in achieving a degree of independence - to drive a car, to drop out of school, and to obtain a work permit. Because the environment is created by intelligence that may take it in many different directions, it takes a long time to learn or adapt. Today, many young people are relatively independent after completing high school, while some remain dependent until graduation from college. There are two categories that do not conform to the pattern, namely, children of homeless families and latchkey kids. In both groupings, young children are forced to assume at least some of the adult functions at an early age.

Homeless men, known variously as hobos, bums, vagrants, and nomads, have existed on the fringes of society for a long time. But homeless families are not on the fringe of society because they are comprised of men and women and children. They have an impact on schools, day care centers, missions and shelters, unemployment offices, and society in general. Families become homeless because they lack the financial resources to maintain a residence in the community. Sometimes none of the members are able to find jobs and earn an income, but more often there is underemployment, i.e., the income of all those working is not sufficient to meet expenses for food, shelter, housing, plus other needs. Occasionally an affordable house or apartment is found and the family moves in, but something happens; jobs are lost, rents are increased, and they are homeless again. Among ethnic and racial minorities and small religious sects, there are short-term opportunities to move in with relatives or neighbors, but overcrowded conditions are rarely satisfactory, so they move on. Part of the daily existence over a period of time will be spent living in vacant buildings, automobiles, fields and even on the sidewalk. Homeless family members lack proper diet, receive little or no health care, are subject to numerous diseases, and also serve as disease carriers. They are subjected to beatings, rapes, the theft of their few possessions, and an environment of squalor.

Young children from homeless families will often be registered in kindergarten, but attendance will be irregular. The probability of dropping out or transferring is high. It is unlikely that young children will be found in child care centers or nursery schools, especially if any fee is charged. It is not uncommon that children from homeless families will come to school without clean clothes and perhaps without bathing very often. Some are shy and withdrawn and reluctant to make friends. One of the identifying traits is an extreme degree of fatigue and the tendency to fall asleep. Symptoms of hunger are often present, to the point of licking crumbs off the floor. Inasmuch as they come from no specific neighborhood, there is usually an absence of playmates and friends.

Johnathan Kozol states there is a tremendous increase in the number of homeless children since 1980. He also says the poverty rate has jumped the most for black children under six. Homeless families, including their children, are a part of a larger social problem -

continuing poverty - that is unresolved. In fact, it has not been faced by the federal government, and only to a slight degree, by states and local communities. For this reason, the teacher who encounters children from these circumstances is very limited in the ability to work with them. The child can be permitted to rest as much as possible when the need is apparent. The teacher should make sure each child participates in any snacks or meals, even if payment has not been made when there is a fee. The homeless child needs to be made welcome and encouraged to participate as much as possible in group activities. The self-concept of children from homeless families is sometimes poor because they can't talk about things other children can. There may be concern that differences from others means they are "bad" or doing something wrong. In some cases, they may be teased or condemned by other children, reflecting the attitudes of their parents toward "lazy" or "worthless" people. The child with a poor self-concept may become aggressive as a defense mechanism. The teacher must remember that homeless children attending kindergarten are often having their first peer group experience and that social adaptation to group activities takes time.

Latchkey Kids

Latchkey kids are children who have a key to their home because there will not be anyone there when they return after school. The term also encompasses, incorrectly, those children who return home to an empty house but they have no key - they are locked out. "Latchkey kids" is the popular term, however, self-care is a more professional term. These children can be of kindergarten age, but the number increases for each age group. This phenomenon began with the increase in working wives and mothers after World War II, and has grown rapidly in recent years. The National Institute of Child Health and Human Development reported that in 1988, 2.4 million children, or seven percent of the children between the ages of five and thirteen, were not supervised by an adult after school. Child Development specialists suspect the number is considerably greater. A 1984 population survey found over 230,000 children, ages 5 to 7, were in self or sibling care after school, some for three hours or more (Hofferth, 1989).

There are several patterns of latchkey children that exist; the only child who comes home alone and has access to the house, two or more children with a key and the oldest is in charge, and one or more children who come home to a locked house. The latter play in the yard, go to neighbors, or spend time at a playground or someplace away from the house. The children who enter the home are sometimes charged with cleaning the house, preparing meals, and supervising younger children and pets, if any. Any of the children in these categories are without adult supervision for several hours. In most cases, they have a number to call in an emergency, but little else to guide them through new situations

(Nichols & Schilit, 1988).

The child's safety is a critical issue for those children who lack adult supervision. Children who are unattended should be given rules that will lessen the dangers for them. The parents are responsible for providing these rules and being sure their child observes them in their absence.

Children can be checked by others if a phone is available. Some communities have organized groups to provide this service, sometimes in conjunction with the public schools.

With regard to age, the younger the child the less the child can cope alone, allowing for an individual child's abilities. Children six and under lack the maturity to care for younger children.

The teacher who works with latchkey kids and/or children from homeless families is likely to encounter an unusual mixture of maturity and immaturity. Such children have responsibilities and are faced with conditions that are normally limited to much older children. On the other hand, they have not had the everyday experiences associated with young children. Play opportunities and playthings may be a minor or even missing aspect of their lives. These children are not necessarily unhappy, nor do they feel deprived. Their feelings toward their parents is likely to be positive; in fact, they often wish their parents were happier or freer to do things they discuss in the evenings.

Peer regulations, on the other hand, will sometimes be difficult, because homeless and latchkey children have experiences that are incompatible with those of other children. Communication and sharing can be difficult. These two groups of children have little opportunity to be together outside of school. Teachers may also have a difficult time relating to such children if they have no previous experience with them. It is important that teachers and others who work with the homeless child and the latchkey kid avoid evaluative or critical comments on their life styles. It is in order to be alert to adjustment problems in the school setting and to dangers on the outside. Research on the impact of young children being alone for prolonged periods of time is lacking because this pattern is relatively new. However, there are dangers of abuse from people the child knows. A poor diet, handling of guns and electrical appliances, and sexual experimenting are some other areas of concern. The capability of young children to cope with attacks or other emergencies which threaten the home or younger siblings is open to question. Homeless and latchkey kids lack the usual degree of supervision so they are not corrected in error of judgment or interpretation in their daily life. It is this guidance at the time of occurrence that is so crucial for a sound sexual development.

ABORTION - LEGAL, CONTROVERSIAL, AND CHANGING

The practice of abortion has existed throughout the known history of man, but there have been a variety of interpretations placed upon it. Aborting the fetus has been carried out for health reasons, for personal convenience, for economic causes, but the most common reason is to prevent the birth of an unwanted child. Both married and unmarried women have sought abortions in every era and some studies have indicated that until recently, a slight majority were performed on married women. In many past civilizations, abortion co-existed with infanticide (the killing of newborn children, usually female) and neither was looked upon as evil. Early Christians then began to stress the sacredness of life. They also had a need for people, so they developed an obligation to reproduce, and simultaneously condemned both abortion and infanticide, but the Western world was slow to accept such restrictions. The desire for abortions remained fairly strong, so the practice continued with varying degrees of acceptance by churches, medical groups, social workers, and the general public until the present time.

In the United States, abortion became increasingly accepted as the desire for smaller families intensified after the depression of the 1930s. Population experts also began to write about overpopulation, the consequences of a baby boom, shortages of food and water, and economists also emphasized a higher standard of living. Abortion remained a common, but concealed practice throughout the country, especially in the urban areas, until 1973. That year, the U.S. Supreme Court virtually abolished all existing laws that restricted abortion in the Roe vs. Wade decision. It declared that during the first trimester, the decision to have an abortion was strictly between a woman and her physician. During the second trimester, the state could impose regulations relating to health, and during the third trimester, laws prohibiting abortion were permissible, except when it was necessary for the preservation of the health or life of the mother, including her mental health.

During the 1980s, the topic of abortion became considerably more controversial. The Supreme Court delivered a decision that upheld a Missouri law requiring that doctors determine whether a fetus is viable at 20 weeks (Missouri law bans the abortion of viable fetuses), permitting the banning of tax money for abortion counseling, and placing a restriction on the use of public monies in relation to abortion. The significance of the decision of the Supreme Court is that states are freer to make rulings on abortions, including new restrictions. As a consequence, every state is now involved in an evaluation of its current laws affecting abortion and whether to make changes in the present position. Political candidates are challenged to state their position on the issue; church congregations have split as to what their official position should be; and picketing, violence, and arson have occurred at clinics where abortions are believed to have taken place.

During 1990, the Supreme Court has agreed to hear two cases that are concerned with teenage abortion and parental consent, one from Ohio and one from Minnesota. Teenage abortion and questions of permission have become a major focus in the abortion issue in recent months. The right of the teenager to privacy and the right of the parent to know about their child's pregnancy and decision to abort are the critical concerns. With more than a million pregnancies among teenage girls each year and almost half choosing abortion as a solution, the court decisions will have great impact regardless of the direction they may go. From the teenage girls' point of view, they do not want their parents involved for several reasons, namely, the parents will be embarrassed, they will be negative or non-supportive, or the girls are already estranged from their parents. Many teenage girls who become pregnant are from troubled homes, and in some cases, may have been sexually abused by one or more of the parents and/or family members. The parents claim they have a right to be involved in the lives of their children and other factors are irrelevant.

Many women's groups have supported abortion in general as a matter of a woman's right to control what happens to her body, while anti-abortion groups assert that abortion is taking a life and is wrong. Public opinion polls reveal that a large majority of Americans favor abortion under certain conditions, but the issue produces mixed feeling for many people. Increased information about the nature of conception and improved techniques of birth control have reduced the number of abortions in recent years in relation to total births, but the number is still substantial. This is true in part, because birth control techniques are not yet 100 percent effective, partly because they are not always used correctly or consistently; and it is also true that some people reject the use of most or all birth control techniques for personal or moral reasons. It might be noted that many of those who oppose abortion are vigorous critics of most birth control methods as well.

One of the possible consequences of increasing the restrictions on abortion could be an increase in sterilization of both men and women. According to the National Center for Health Statistics, more than one-third of all sexually active American women, aged 18 to 44, had been sterilized by 1987. Among the methods of birth control used in 1987, 36 percent involved sterilization, 32 percent took a contraceptive pill, 16 percent used condoms, while no other technique was over five percent. Eight percent of the women utilized no birth control procedure.

A newer and better birth control method is being considered by the

Food and Drug Administration. The Norplant hormone implant is 98 percent effective, would reduce teenage pregnancy, and also ease the problem of forgetting to take the pill. This method uses the hormone, progestogen, which is placed in tiny rods and implanted in a woman's upper arm in a simple surgical procedure. It prevents pregnancy for five years and can be removed when pregnancy is desired. The implant is being unanimously recommended for use in the United States by the advisory committee for the FDA.

A new dimension has been added to the abortion issue with the emergence of the AIDS disease, namely, the question of mandatory testing of pregnant women and the further question of what should be done if the prospective mother tests positive. If nothing is done, there is the possibility of a diseased child and a dying mother, both of whom will need extensive medical, social, and financial assistance. The alternatives at present are to treat the disease with inadequate methods, or to abort the fetus. In a recent report, a task force of the World Health Organization noted a 95 percent success rate with drug-induced, non-surgical abortions. The experimental treatment involves the sequential administration of two medicines. One of the medicines in the combined therapy is a prostaglandin, which stimulates the uterus to contract, and the other is the French abortion "pill" RU 486. It works by blocking the action of the sex hormone, progesterone, which is necessary to the development of the fetus and its attachment to the uterus. At the present time, RU 486 is banned from the United States and is one more pawn in the controversy over abortion and its many ramifications.

As mentioned above, the underlying cause of most abortions is that a child is not wanted, but there are many reasons behind this attitude. Many married women do not wish to disrupt their current lifestyle with a child or another child if they have a family, at least at the present time. Some do not believe they can afford the cost and inconvenience of a pregnancy and delivery. Unmarried women are sometimes not in a position to care for a child. In some cases, the father-to-be has rejected marriage and/or the fetus. There are instances where the pregnancy is the result of rape or incest and a child is considered unacceptable. The presence of genetic defects or deficiencies as uncovered by amniocentesis may also result in a decision to abort. These are real and important beliefs to millions of men and women, so it is unlikely that abortion will disappear. One additional concern of many is that if the restrictions on legal abortion are increased, or it is made illegal, doctors will perform them outside the office or hospital, or a number of non-professionals will begin performing them as was true in the past. Males have also expressed concern about their rights in any decision to abort a fetus, because they would ultimately be the father if the birth is allowed to occur.

It is probably impossible to adequately explain the nature of abortion, the reasons for abortion, or what happens to the fetus, to a young child. Death is not really meaningful to a young person, except that a given individual is no longer around to play with or to talk to. It is unlikely that parents or other adults would discuss a prospective abortion with a small child, or even in the presence of a young child, but it is possible to be overheard. One real danger is a linkage of abortion with unwanted and unloved children, and most children have concerns in this area. What should an adult do if a child asks, "Did you ever think about me this way?" The basic approach is the same one that can and should be employed frequently when explaining difficult situations to a pre-school child, namely, to emphasize love and concern for him or her and to answer honestly in terms that the child can grasp and that will not have to be retracted later. The self-development of a little boy is truly enhanced when he feels that he is wanted as a boy in that family at that point in time.   Similarly, a little girl needs reassurance and reinforcement that it is great that she is a girl and an important part of the group and is really loved.

SOME FINAL THOUGHTS

To start a book is always difficult; to end it is even more so. There seem to be more things that need to be said. To omit ideas of importance would be terrible, but so would belaboring points that have already been made. Hopefully, we have resolved these worries by concluding with a gentle warning, a positive viewpoint, and a hope for the future.

The gentle warning is to all those who work with young children - be ever aware that you cannot avoid communicating to the young child. You communicate by speaking and also by not speaking; by what you say and what you don't say. To scold with a smile does not convey the same message as scolding with a frown. Your words may be negated by your actions or they may be reinforced. To say nothing, but to turn away abruptly is a communicative action. The choice of words employed is obviously a critical factor in a message, but the meaning intended by the speaker is not necessarily the meaning received by the listener. It has been emphasized throughout this book that the sexuality of the young child is continually influenced by the people, events, and things as they are experienced.   Children place an interpretation upon them, an interpretation that is based on very limited experience. For a child of five, one year is twenty percent of his or her lifetime. That which is seen and heard must be defined on the basis of those five years of living.

When peers communicate, they can look each other in the eye, but to talk to an adult, children must look up. When a teacher kneels down to the child's level, a different relationship is established than occurs when one remains standing. Many times words and expressions are used which children do not understand fully, if at all; but some kind of communication takes place, including an interpretation of those who spoke and their attitudes toward young children; thus the children attach some degree of importance to that occurrence. The crux of this warning is that those who work with young children need to be constantly alert to the possibility of unsuccessful communication in terms of that which was intended and the unintended consequences of any misunderstandings. It is often not enough to ask, "Do you understand?" It may be necessary to determine what has been understood, even if the child answered the question, "Yes." It is not possible to not communicate, but it is very possible to not communicate the message that is intended.

Secondly, it is hard to be anything but positive about young children when working with them. They have an eagerness to learn, to do new things, to repeat old things, to have more experiences, all of which is most impressive and challenging. There is an appreciation of little things, and a "joie de vie" that is delightful to see and be around. The mistakes they make and those made by others are quickly forgotten and, therefore, can easily be overcome. The most positive aspects of this ability to forgive and forget is that those children who are physically and/or sexually abused are not scarred for life. They can proceed to newer and better things as soon as they receive love and attention. The child who is deprived or denied accurate or complete information about the nature of the human body, its functioning, and its naturalness, can promptly go on about the business of growing up more wisely as soon as the proper guidance becomes available. Young children have no preconceived ideas about good and bad, right and wrong, or the decency and honesty of people so they can respond quickly to either correct or incorrect information.

Those who teach and supervise young children have the opportunity to contribute to their sound sexual development without creating feelings of guilt or establishing conflicts between children and their parents and playmates. If trust is established with the children and honest communication with the parents or guardians, a sound foundation is established on which the future can be based. Healthy sexual development requires that children be instructed, guided, and corrected; these can be accomplished as forms of loving and caring. When teachers have bad days (and they do), or when they make a mistake, children will also correct and guide, because they too love and care. To maintain a feeling of positiveness does not require any attempts to probe the deepest feelings of children. What the child really feels as he goes through his activities each day can rarely be determined by anyone else and sometimes not even the child knows how he or she is feeling down deep. Helping develop the sexuality means helping the child have a good sense about himself or herself as a person and as a member of various groups. It does not require analysis in depth; that must be left for experts. In most situations, parents and teachers can achieve wonderful results by working to establish an informed child who is comfortable alone and in groups; the child is ready, willing, and able.

Finally, the wonderful qualities of young children makes one wish they would never have to experience the negatives of the real world of which they will increasingly become a part. We would hope that the generations of the future could be spared the agonies of AIDS, the degradation of drug addiction, the miseries of alcoholism, and the suffering and despair of poverty and unemployment. However, these aspects of society will not be resolved or eliminated by hoping. Some children are exposed to some of the many ramifications of the above-mentioned, as well as other problems before they reach school age. In most cases, young children suffer no permanent damage if relief comes early and consistently over time. The resiliency discussed above is a great asset, but there are children who can be helped only with a major effort and a few who are almost beyond help. Some mental and physical diseases and injuries can be treated only by specialists at great expense and with limited chances of improvement. Generally, teachers and parents of young children can reduce the chances of their charges experiencing these societal failings by helping build a sexuality that can cope with confidence with the inevitable problems that lie ahead.

This book has stressed the sexuality of young children as an integration of personal traits and experiences, thus enabling young children to understand and appreciate their own being and to prepare for the requirements of living and working with an ever increasing number of people. Parents and teachers play the major role in achieving a sound sexuality for children. For them to be most effective, they too must come to grips with their own sexuality and strive to strengthen it as they simultaneously work to assist the young children. One manifestation of a strong sexuality is the willingness to accept challenges with confidence; another is the recognition that some challenges also require the help of experts and professionals in those areas where the parent's or teacher's training and experience is not enough. In the final sense, helping young children build a strong sexuality means helping them enjoy being children who are also willing to grow up.

QUESTIONS FOR DISCUSSION

1. Explore the impact of infertility, adoption, and abortion on each other. How do the legal, social, and moral implications of any one affect the other two?

2. What is the influence of artificial insemination, including IVF, on infertility, adoption, and abortion? How do people's attitudes or beliefs about these various situations and procedures affect their attitudes and beliefs about young children and how they should be reared?

3. Should a child delivered by a surrogate mother be informed of that fact at any time? If so, when? What are a teacher's responsibilities if such a situation becomes known by the class?

4. Compare and evaluate the home situation of a young child being reared by a single parent who is heterosexual with that of a child being reared by a homosexual? How important are the differences, if any?

5. Are latchkey kids likely to have any special problems while in the pre-school setting? What are the teacher's responsibilities? Should a teacher become involved in the financial or social problems of the parents of the children in the group? Explain.

6. If a young child asks about abortion, should a teacher attempt to explain it, ignore the question, or refer it to the parents? What are the major considerations for the teacher who attempts to explain abortion? If a child persists, can it be ignored? Should personal opinions and beliefs enter into any classroom discussion of abortion? Can they be kept out?

CHAPTER REFERENCES

Bozett, F.W. ed. (1987). Gay and lesbian parents. New York: Praeger.

Brenes, M.E., N. Eisenberg & G. Helmstadter (1985). Sex role development of pre-schoolers from two-parent and one-parent families. Merrill-Palmer Quarterly, 31: 33-46.

Briggs, B.A. & C.M. Walters (1985). Single-father families. Young Children, 40: 23-27.

Green, R. (1978). Sexual identity of 37 children raised by homosexual and transsexual parents. American Journal of Psychiatry, 135: 692-697.

Hofferth, S.L. (1989). Parental choice of self-care for school-age children. Journal of Marriage and the Family, 51: 65-77.

Kozol, J. (1988). Rachel and her children: homeless families in America. New York: Crown.

Nichols, A.W. & R. Schilit (1988). Telephone support for latchkey children. Child Welfare, 67: 49-59.

Schulenberg, J. (1985). The complete guide to gay parenting. New York: Doubleday.

GLOSSARY

ABORTION - The termination of a pregnancy by the removal or expulsion of the contents of the uterus. This may occur through medical intervention or spontaneously (miscarriage).

AIDS - Acquired Immune Deficiency Syndrome. See STD.

AMNIOCENTESIS - A procedure to remove amniotic fluid which surrounds the fetus in the uterus for the purpose of detecting various characteristics of the fetus, including diseases of an undesirable nature.

ARTIFICIAL INSEMINATION - The injection of semen into the vagina or uterus by means of a syringe. This procedure is employed to fertilize a woman who desires to become pregnant, but has been unable to do so by means of sexual intercourse.

BISEXUALITY - Sexual attraction to people of one's own sex and to those of the opposite sex, not necessarily on an even ratio.

BONDING - An attachment between parent and child that begins at birth and develops during the first eighteen months of a child's life. Some theorize that this attachment is crucial for the soundest sexual development.

CERVIX - The lower end of the uterus through which the sperm pass unless preventive measures are taken. See CONTRACEPTION.

CHILD MOLESTER - A person, usually a man, who seeks sexual satisfaction from physical contact with children. The molesting may involve touching and caressing or it may involve the sexual organs and/or oral, anal, or sexual intercourse.

CONTRACEPTION - The use of devices such as condoms, IUD's, birth control pills, vaginal spermicides, diaphragms, and douches which are designed to prevent the sperm and egg from making contact and becoming fertilized. Actions such as withdrawal and natural family planning are also included.

EMBRYO - The fertilized egg becomes an embryo after one week. See FETUS.

FEMALE - A human being who can be impregnated by the sperm of the male, carry the resulting embryo, then fetus, to the point of delivering a human offspring. She also has the capability to nurse the newborn child. See MALE.

FEMININE - Pertains to the attitudes and behaviors expected of a female in a specific social system. Varies from culture to culture and from one historical period to another. See MASCULINE.

FERTILIZATION - The union of an egg (ovum) and sperm cell resulting in conception. The union must occur in the Fallopian tube during the fertile period of less than one week each month.

FETUS - The fertilized embryo from the beginning of the third month after conception until birth. See EMBRYO.

GENDER - The general term for the two sexes; male and female. Some students are beginning to argue that two is not enough, because of the great number of variations among both sexes.

GENDER IDENTITY - The awareness of being male or female. It is learned from birth by the treatment afforded the child. Any inconsistency may create confusion as to the appropriate gender on the part of a young child. Also known as SEXUAL IDENTITY.

GENITALS - The external sexual and/or reproductive organs of both male and female humans. Also known as genitalia.

GIFT - Gamete Intra Fallopian Transfer. GIFT involves the surgical removal of eggs from a woman's ovary, mixing them with the male sperm, and replacing the eggs back in the Fallopian Tube where natural fertilization takes place.

HETEROSEXUAL - A human whose overt sex behavior is directed toward persons of the opposite sex. See HOMOSEXUAL and BISEXUAL.

HIV - Human Immunodeficiency Virus. The HIV virus causes AIDS by infecting certain cells of the immune system. Not everyone with the virus becomes ill, but they can transmit the disease.

INCEST - Sexual intercourse between blood relatives closer than permitted by law.

INFERTILITY - The inability of a female to become pregnant or of a male to impregnate a female. The causes are many and varied and often can be corrected.

IVF - In Vitro Fertilization. The fertilization of an egg and male sperm outside the woman's body. The resulting embryo is later transferred back to the woman's womb. Also known as Test Tube Babies.

LESBIAN - A female homosexual.

MALE - A human being with external genitalia including a penis, and scrotum. Normally, a male can generate sperm which can be utilized to impregnate a female. See FEMALE.

MASCULINE - Pertains to the attitudes and expectations of a male in a specific social system. Varies from culture to culture and historical era to era. See FEMININE.

MASTURBATION - Self-stimulation of the genitals by either males or females; for the purpose of orgasm by adults.

ORGASM - A climax achieved as a result of sexual stimulation; resulting in a release of sexual tensions.

OVUM - The reproductive cell produced in the ovary of a female and discharged monthly during ovulation, unless united with a male sperm resulting in fertilization. Also known as egg.

PEDOPHILE - An adult who seeks to engage in sexual activity with children; may be male or female, homosexual or heterosexual in orientation.

PENIS - The male sex organ through which sperm are discharged.

PORNOGRAPHY - Sexually explicit material designed to stimulate sexual arousal. The specific determination of what is pornographic is widely disputed in religious and legal areas.

SEXUAL IDENTITY - See GENDER IDENTITY.

SEX ROLE - The behaviors engaged in by a person because they are believed to be appropriate and representative for their sex (gender). The behaviors vary continuously with age, and are different for various cultural groupings around the world.

SEXUAL INTERCOURSE - A relationship between male and female in which the penis enters the vagina, regardless of position of their bodies.

SEXUALITY - The totality of one's sexual nature, including behavior, attitudes, and relationships with others.

STD - Sexually Transmitted Disease. Diseases such as AIDS, syphilis, gonorrhea, chlamydia, herpes, among others, which are transmitted through sexual relations - intercourse, oral and anal contacts, and any other physical contacts.

SPERM - The male reproductive cell produced in the testes and ejaculated as part of the semen during orgasm. See OVUM.

STERILITY - The inability of male or female to reproduce. See INFERTILITY.

STERILIZATION - Any procedure or occurrence that causes an individual to become incapable of producing offspring. The most common surgeries are vasectomy for men and tubal ligation for women. Sterilizing diseases include gonorrhea and endometriosis.

TRANSSEXUAL - A person who feels that he or she is of the opposite gender, resulting in confused gender identity.

TRANSVESTITE - A person who has a compulsion to dress in the clothes of and to impersonate the behavior of a person of the opposite sex. May achieve sexual gratification while cross-dressed.

UTERUS - A hollow muscular organ in the female that keeps and nourishes the fetus during pregnancy, and helps expel the baby during delivery. Also known as womb.

VAGINA - A muscular tube connecting the female external genitalia (vulva) with the cervix. See SEXUAL INTERCOURSE.

RESOURCES

FOR YOUNG CHILDREN

Andrews, C. and Schepp, D. (1984)
How babies are made.
Boston, MA: Little Brown

Bassett, K. (1987) (4th ed.)
My very own special body book.
Redding, CA: Hawthorn Press

Freeman, L. (1983)
It's my body.
Everett, WA: Planned Parenthood of Snohormish Co.

Gordon, S. and Gordon, J. (1982)
Did the sun shine before you were born?
Fayetteville, NY: Ed.-U- Press (Ages 3-7)

Moglia, R., Welbourne - Moglia, A. and Hoffner, A. (1989)
How to talk to your child about AIDS.
SIECUS: New York University, New York, NY

Quackenbush, M. and Villarreal, S. (1988)
Does AIDS hurt? educating young children about AIDS.
Santa Cruz, CA: Network Publications

Schoen, M. (1989)
Belly buttons are navals
Buffalo, NY
Prometheus Books (Ages 3-8)

Teach A Bodies (Anatomically Correct Dolls)
2544 Boyd Avenue
Fort Worth, TX 76109

FOR ADULTS

Bach, G. (1985)
Are you still my mother?
New York: Warner Books

Dickman, I.R. (1982)
Winning the battle for sex education.
New York: SIECAS Report

Griffin, C., Wirth, M. and Wirth, A. (1986)
Beyond acceptance.
Englewood Cliffs, NJ: Prentice Hall.

Koop, E. (1988) Surgeon General and the Center for Disease Control
Understanding AIDS.
Washington, DC: HHS Publication No. (CDC), HHS 88-8404

Levine, J. (1977)
Who will raise the children? New options for fathers and mothers.
New York: Bantam Books

Lyman, M. (1984 rev.)
Sex education at home: a guide for parents.
Syracuse, NY: Planned Parenthood Center of Syracuse

Rowdle, W. (1989) May
AIDS prevention guide.
American Responds to AIDS,
Department of Health and Human Services,
Public Health Service, Center for Disease Control,
Atlanta, GA

SIECUS - Sex Information and Education Council of the U.S.
130 West 42nd St., Suite 2500
New York, NY 10036

Staff. (1983) NAEYC
How to choose a good early childhood program.
Washington, DC

INFORMATION

There are many agencies and organizations that give help and information about sexuality in addition to available literature and other audio-visual materials. Schools, especially universities and colleges, libraries, churches, hospitals and various service groups offer services and seminars on topics that relate to sexuality.

The phone directory is also useful in locating a source to provide help. Both the white and yellow pages may contain the necessary information

National and local crisis hot-lines are often a quick way to locate a source for help. The workers, paid or volunteer, are well trained and some hot-lines operate on a 24 hour basis.

HOT-LINES

Abortion - 800-772-9100

AIDS (National) - 800-342-AIDS

Child Abuse - 800-422-4453

Child Care
National Association for the Education of Young Children - 800-424-2460

Gay and Lesbian Crises Line - 800-767-4297 (Mon - Fri 5-10 PM)

BIBLIOGRAPHY AND READING LIST

Allen, C. (1980). Daddy's girl. New York: Wyndom Press.

Armstrong, L. (1978). Kiss daddy goodnight. New York: Hawthorn Press.

Arnstein, H. (1967). Your growing child and sex: a parent's guide to the sexual development, education, attitudes, and behaviors of the child. . . from infancy through adolescence. Indianapolis: Bobbs Merrill.

Bell, A., Weinberg, M. & Hammersmith, S. (1982). Sexual preference: its development in men and women. Bloomington, IN: Indiana University Press.

Berger, S. (1970). Sex education of the young child. Young Children, 25: 266-267.

Bettelheim, B. (1987). A good enough parent. New York: Alfred A. Knopf.

Boat, B. & Everson, M. (1988). Use of anatomical dolls among professionals in sexual abuse evaluations. Child Abuse and Neglect, 12: 171-179.

Boat, B. & Everson, M. (1988). Interviewing young children with anatomical dolls. Child Welfare, 67: 337-352.

Bozett, F. (ed.) (1987). Gay and lesbian parents. New York: Praeger.

Brazelton, T. (1981). On becoming a family: the growth of attachment. New York: Dell.

Brazelton, T. (1983). Infants and mothers (rev. ed.). New York: Delacorte Press.

Brenes, M., Eisenberg, N. & Helmstadter, G. (1985). Sex role development of pre-schoolers from two parent and one parent families. Merrill-Palmer Quarterly, 31: 33-46.

Briggs, B. & Walters, C. (1985). Single father families. Young Children, 40: 23-27.

Burgess, A., Grath, N., Halstrom, L. & Sgroc, S. (1978). Sexual assault: for children and adolescents. Lexington, MA: Lexington Books.

188

Burns, R. (1986). <u>Child development: a text for the caring professions</u>. New York: Nichols Publishing Company.

Butler, S. (1978). <u>Conspiracy of silence: the trauma of incest</u>. San Francisco: New Glide Publications.

Calderone, M. (1966). The development of healthy sexuality. <u>Journal of Health, Physical Education, and Recreation</u>, <u>37</u>: 28-32.

Calderone, M. (1983). Fetal erection and its message to us. <u>SIECUS Report</u>, <u>11</u>, (5/6): 9-10.

Calderone, M. (1985). Adolescent sexuality: elements and genesis. <u>Pediatrics</u>, <u>76</u>: 699-703.

Calderone, M. & Johnson, E. (1981). <u>The family book about sexuality</u>. New York: Harper and Row.

Caldwell, B. (1983). How can we educate the American public about the child care profession. <u>Young Children</u>, <u>38</u>: 11-17.

Constantine, L. & Martinson, F. (1981). <u>Children and self: new findings, new perspectives</u>. Boston: Little, Brown and Company.

Cowan, C. & Cowan, P. (1988). Who does what when partners become parents: implications for men, women, and marriage. <u>Marriage and Family Review</u>, <u>12</u>: 105-131.

Decker, C. (1988). <u>Children, the early years</u>. South Holland, IL: Goodheart-Wilcox Co.

D'Evelyn, K. (1970). <u>Developing mentally healthy children</u>. Washington, DC: Study Action Publication from the American Association of Elementary, Kindergarten, Nursery Educators.

Elam, A. & Walters, L. (1985). The father and the law. <u>American Behavioral Scientist</u>, <u>29</u>: 78-111.

Elkin, F. (1989). <u>The child and society: the process of socialization</u>, (5th ed.) New York: Random House.

Elwell, M. (1979). Sexually assaulted children and their families. <u>Social Casework</u>, <u>60</u>: 227-235.

Essa, E. (1990). <u>A practical guide to solving preschool behavior problems</u>, (2nd ed.). Albany, NY: Delmar.

Finkelhor, D. (1979). <u>Sexually victimized children</u>. New York: Free Press.

Finkelhor, D. (1984). <u>Child sexual abuse: new theory and research</u>. New York: Free Press.

Finkelhor, D. (1984). How widespread is child sexual abuse? <u>Children Today</u>, <u>13</u>: 18-20.

Finkelhor, D. & Williams, L. (1988). <u>Nursery crimes: sexual abuse in day care</u>. Newbury Park, CA: Sage Publications.

Floge, L. (1985). The dynamics of child-care use and some implications for women's employment. <u>Journal of Marriage and the Family</u>, <u>47</u>: 143-154.

Gagnon, J. (ed.) (1977). <u>Human sexualities</u>. Glenview, IL: Scott, Foresman.

Gale, J., Thompson, R., Moral, T. & Sack, W. (1988). Sexual abuse in young children: its clinical presentation and characteristic patterns. <u>Child Abuse and Neglect</u>, <u>12</u>: 163-170.

Galinsky, E. & Hooks, W. (1977). <u>The new extended family: day care that works</u>. Boston: Houghton Mifflin.

Galinsky, E. & David, J. (1988). <u>The preschool years: family strategies that work - from experts and parents</u>. New York: Times Books.

Godow, A. (1982). <u>Human sexuality</u>. St. Louis: Mosby.

Gold, S. (1986). <u>When children invite abuse: a search for answers when love is not enough</u>. Eugene, OR: Fern Ridge Press.

Gordon, M. (1989). The family environment of sexual abuse: a comparison of natural and stepfather abuse. <u>Child Abuse and Neglect</u>, <u>13</u>: 121-130.

Gordon, S. & Gordon, J. (1986). <u>Raising a child conservatively in a sexually permissive world</u>. New York: Simon and Schuster.

Grams, A. (1970). <u>Sex education: a guide for teachers</u> (2nd ed.). Danville, IL: Interstate Printers and Publishers.

Green, R. (1978). Sexual identity of 37 children raised by homosexual and transsexual parents. <u>American Journal of Psychiatry</u>, <u>135</u>: 692-697.

Green, R. (1987). <u>The "sissy boy syndrome" and the development of homosexuality</u>. New Haven: Yale University Press.

Greenberg, D. (1988). The construction of homosexuality. Chicago: University of Chicago Press.

Greif, G. (1985). Single fathers rearing children. Journal of Marriage and the Family, 47: 185-191.

Grimm, D. (1987). Toward a theory of gender. American Behavioral Scientist, 31: 66-85.

Herman, J. (1981). Father daughter incest. Cambridge, MA: Harvard University Press.

Hill, S. & Barnes, B. (1982). Young children and their families. Lexington, MA: Lexington, Books.

Hofferth, S. (1989). Parental choice of self-care for school age children. Journal of Marriage and the Family, 51: 65-77.

Hofferth, S. (1989). What is the demand for and supply of child care in the United States? A public policy report. Young Children, 44: 28-33.

Kadushin, A. & Martin, J. (1981). Child abuse: an international event. New York: Columbia University Press.

Kessler, S. & McKenna, W. (1978). Gender: an ethnomethodological approach. Chicago: University of Chicago Press.

Klaus, M. & Kennell, J. (1976). Maternal infant bonding. St. Louis: Mosby.

Kozol, J. (1988). Rachael and her children; homeless families in America. New York: Crown.

Kuhn, D., Nash, S. & Brucker, L. (1978). Sex role concepts of two and three year olds. Child Development, 49: 445-451.

Leach, P. (1987). The first six months. New York: Alfred A. Knopf.

Leavitt, R. & Eheart, B. (1985). Toddler day care. Lexington, MA: Lexington Books.

Leslie, G. (1979). The family in social context (4th ed.). New York: Oxford University Press.

Levine, M. (1968). What to tell your child about sex. New York: E.P. Dutton.

Lewis, R. (1985-86). Men's changing roles in the family. Marriage and Family Review, 9: nos. 3/4. (entire issue).

Looft, W. (1971). Sex education for parents. The Journal for School Health, 41: 433-437.

Lueptow, L. (1984). Adolescent sex roles and social change. New York: Columbia University Press.

Maccoby, E. & Jacklin, C. (1974). The psychology of sex differences. Stanford, CA: Stanford University Press.

Macklin, E. (1989). AIDS and families. Marriage and Family Review, 13: 1-271. Nos. 1/2.

Maltz, W. & Holman, B. (1987). Incest and sexuality. Lexington, MA: Lexington Books.

Masters, J. (1986). Forum feedback. Playboy, 33: 42-46.

Masters, W., Johnson, V. & Kolodny, R. (1988). Crisis: heterosexual behavior in the age of AIDS. New York: Grove Press.

Mead, M. (1975). Bisexuality: what it is all about. Redbook, Jan.

Miller, J. (1986). Toward a new psychology of women. Boston: Beacon Press.

Money, J. (1980). Love and love sickness: the science of sex, gender differences, and pair bonding. Baltimore, MD: Johns Hopkins University Press.

Money, J. & Tucker, P. (1975). Sexual signatures: on being a man or a woman. Boston: Little Brown.

Morgan, E. (1989). Talking with parents when concerns come up. Young Children, 44: 52-56.

Morrison, G. (1990). The world of child development: conception to adolescence. Albany, NY: Delmar.

Neal, A., Groat, H. & Wicks, J. (1989). Attitudes about having children: a study of 600 couples in the early years of marriage. Journal of Marriage and the Family, 51: 313-327.

Nichols, A. & Schilit, R. (1988). Telephone support for latch-key children. Child Welfare, 67: 49-59.

Phillips, D. & Whitebook, M. (1986). Who are the child care workers? Young Children, 41: 14-20.

Pogrebin, L. (1980). Growing up free: raising your child in the 80's. New York: McGraw-Hill.

Ramos, S. (1979). The complete book of child custody. New York: P.G. Putnam Sons.

Reed, S. (1988). Children with AIDS. Phi Deltan Kappan (Special Report), 69: K1-K12

Rush, F. (1980). The best kept secret: sexual abuse of children. Englewood Cliffs, NJ: Prentice-Hall.

Sanford, L. (1980). The silent children: a parent's guide to the prevention of sexual child abuse. Garden City, NY: Anchor Press.

Schenk, V. & Gusec, J. (1986). A comparison of prosocial behavior of children with and without day care experience. Merrill-Palmer Quarterly, 31: 231-240.

Schetky, D. & Green, A. (1988). Child pornography and prostitution. New York: Brunner Mazel Publishers.

Schoen, Mark. (1989). Belly buttons are navals. Santa Cruz, CA: Network Publications.

Schulenberg, J. (1985). The complete guide to gay parenting. New York: Doubleday.

Segal, J. & Segal, Z. (1985). Growing up smart and happy. New York: McGraw-Hill.

Shiff, E. (ed.) (1987). Experts advise parents: a guide to raising loving responsible children. New York: Delacorte Press.

SIECUS (1970) Sexuality and man. New York: Charles Scribner Sons.

Spock, B. (1988). Dr. Spock on parenting: sensible advise from America's most trusted child care expert. New York: Simon and Schuster.

Stream, H. (1988). Effects of childhood sexual abuse on the psychosocial functioning of adults. Social Work, 33: 465-467

Staff, SIECUS (1970). Sexuality and man. New York: Charles Scribner's Sons.

Staff, Child Study Association of America/Wel-Met (1974). What to tell your child about sex. (rev. ed.) New York: J. Aronson.

Staff, Committee for Children (1988). Talking about touching: a personal safety curriculum. Seattle, WA:

Swan, H. (1984). Happy Bear: teaching pre-school children about sexual abuse. Topeka, KS: Kansas Child Abuse Prevention Council.

Tronick, E. & Adamson, L. (1980). Babies as people: new finding on our social beginnings. New York: Collier Books.

Wattleton, W. & Keiffer, E. (1986). How to talk with your child about sexuality. Garden City, NY: Doubleday.

White, B. (1989). Gender differences in marital communication. Family Process, 28: 89-106.

Whittlestone, W. (1989). Background to bonding. Child and Family, 19: 84-97.

Williams, W. (1987). Women, men and others. American Behavioral Scientist, 31: 135-141.

Yorburg, B. (1974). Sexual identity: sex roles and social change. New York: John Wiley and Sons.

INDEX